HEAVEN
Help the HOME
the
today

Howard & Jeanne Hendricks

LIFE
JOURNEY

An Imprint of Cook Communications Ministries
Colorado Springs, Colorado

Life Journey® is an imprint of
Cook Communications Ministries, Colorado Springs, CO 80918
Cook Communications, Paris, Ontario
Kingsway Communications, Eastbourne, England

HEAVEN HELP THE HOME TODAY
©2003 by Howard & Jeanne Hendricks

First Printing August 2003
Printed in the United States of America
1 2 3 4 5 6 7 8 9 10 — 10 09 08 07 06 05 04 03

Cover Design: Jeffrey P. Barnes
Cover Photography ©PhotoDisc
Interior Design: Jeffrey P. Barnes

Cataloging-in-Publication Data on file with the Library of Congress
ISBN: 0781438101

Contents

A Starter Kit for a Lasting Legacy

Twenty-nine years ago the first version of this commentary on the Christian home made it into print. Our four children had grown into teens and twenty-somethings. I had enough battle-scars, I thought, to qualify as a knowledgeable author on the subject of family. My own in-house experience, coupled with my intense scrutiny of the Bible, yielded answers—solutions to many problems I wish I had known years earlier.

Then again, more than a decade later, during my early grandfathering experience, I updated these pages because in that short time the world had changed in significant ways. Basic principles from the Bible always remain the same, but the society that impacts family had twisted drastically.

Now, here I am with middle-aged children and grandchildren who are blooming into adulthood. I am classified as "elderly," but the concept of family still has not changed even though I certainly have had major alterations in my own life. For one thing, I had allowed my wife to be the silent partner in the book when in truth she is the "chief operating officer" of our home as well as a recognized, published author. So I vowed that her name would appear on the cover of this third edition.

Once again, the swift current of modern life has presented new challenges to us. Our newest generation breathes toxic air polluted with worsening moral and spiritual decay. It requires rigorous discipline to stay on course with God's prescription for a healthy family. We see it more clearly now than we ever did before.

FEAR OF FAMILY FAILURE

These pages are not the soft conclusions of contented retirees. Every day I step into my classroom of graduate students and interact with tense young parents or with apprehensive singles who fear family failure. Both of us often grapple with the panic of older, discouraged, and disillusioned fathers, mothers, and grandparents. We also hang out with not a few young people who are distressed over their own parents and families. Our personal loss of a daughter and a daughter-in-law, as well as marital difficulties in our children's lives, have stabbed us painfully. Our words grow out of the troubled soil on which we walk.

"Doing" Christian family life in twenty-first-century America is an unprecedented challenge, a declaration of war against forces that flagrantly oppose biblical teaching. Every home exudes a unique aroma, but if we are to accomplish what God intended, we must fly the flag of His kingdom and dedicate ourselves unreservedly to His purposes. We seek to bring our readers a balanced word of encouragement, a starter kit to build the most lasting and satisfying legacy possible.

"The child digs his well in the seashore sand, and the great ocean, miles deep, miles wide, is stirred all through and through to fill it for him." This wisdom fell from the lips of the former president of Moody Bible Institute, Dr. George Sweeting. It summarizes the impact of one family on the world.

Begin with marriage, which God Himself inaugurated. This holy, one-flesh union of one man with one woman forms the framework for an unshakable love commitment enriching their community. With strength and resilience that nothing in the world can equal, a godly home builds a stable society where team loyalty and tough love nourish each family member.

In turn, each child grows to adulthood and leaves to reproduce that caring spirit. It shows up in a humble recognition of God as Creator and Giver of resources: time, money, health, relationships. In a Christian home everything is regarded as a means to glorify God and to enjoy our humanity. If we receive with gratitude, dependent on the Giver, then we can plow a straight furrow and leave a firm foundation for the next generation.

What If We've Already Messed Up?

But what if we did not have an intact home? What if, early on, we did not know about God's love? What if we already messed things up and the family fractured? The principles remain the same, even though there are inevitable consequences. God's mercy and grace is always available to begin again wherever a believer is willing to trust the Great Physician.

Whether our readers are newlyweds just building their nest, or seasoned seniors who bear scars of past personal misfortune, the Bible offers direction, and we propose to seek God's viewpoint wherever we find ourselves. God has placed us in families, a privilege we should never take lightly. We are not suggesting a dark, dour home with eyes and ears closed to the world, but one where every modern invention is considered and dedicated to the overall purpose of enjoying life as God meant it to be. Nothing in all of the world is more attractive than that dot on the map called home, when life is celebrated with fun and exudes warm comfort.

—HOWARD G. HENDRICKS (WITH JEANNE)

CHAPTER ONE

The Christian Home: Now More than Ever!

Unless the LORD builds the house,
They labor in vain who build it.
Psalm 127:1

"I've either got the wrong recipe or the wrong ingredients! I've thrown my whole life into this stew; and if this family isn't the worst mess of rotten goulash I've ever seen! Sometimes I just want to give up."

This bitter blast spurted from Carolyn, twenty years down the holey road of marriage and motherhood. Carolyn grew up going to church and doing all the "right things." At the proper age she married Fred, a "really nice guy," generous, easygoing, and friendly. He was a bit weak, but she helped him make decisions.

When the two kids were born, Fred was gone most of the time in military service, but she managed. She even went to work to help save money for the home they would buy when he got out. She had intended to quit working when Fred got home, but he was restless and unsure of himself so she kept on.

Soon it was apparent that Fred had a drinking problem. Typical for Carolyn, she was patient, understanding, and kept on running the job and the family. Meanwhile, Fred, on and off the job, in and out of hospitals, with and apart from his family, staggered through a decade in search of solid ground.

"He's been living at home for about a year now," reported Carolyn, "and I think he finally knows he's always just a drink away from disaster. He's been doing pretty well, but I'm really worried now. Cari—that's our younger one—told us some time ago that when she graduates from high school next month, she plans to live with her boyfriend at the university. I thought somehow I'd talk her out of it. But I wasn't prepared for last night. When I got home from work, there was her boyfriend's truck, and they were moving all her stuff out of the house. She's just leaving—going to live with that boy! I can't reason with her."

Changes in the culture do not mandate a foundational reorganization of the Christian home.

A toxic air has settled under the roofs of the Carolyns and Freds of our world. It is as if a central heating/air conditioning system were spewing out poisonous gas. The distinctively Christian home (not merely the house where Christians live, but the family where Christ rules) seems to be scarcer than ever.

Should we conclude that the Christian family is a lost cause? Allow the historians to write that the modular family unit of monogamous marriage adhering to Judeo-Christian principles saw its demise in the Western world at the close of the twentieth century? Is it valid to be concerned about the Christian home? Could we, maybe, just toss it out with the next garbage collection?

Hardly! Changes in the culture do not mandate a foundational reorganization of the Christian home. God ordained it; it is here to stay. There are substantial and scriptural reasons that build a compelling and convincing case for the home.

THE BIBLE EXALTS THE FAMILY

Speaking specifically about marriage, sex, and family responsibilities, the Scriptures headline family responsibilities. Blood ties are emphasized in the Old Testament as it traces Abraham's family of faith and expectation of the Messiah. The New Testament introduces Him, Jesus Christ in human flesh, teaching us about life in the Spirit, His Holy Spirit.

We need to understand how prominent the family is in the Bible—and how important a God-centered family is in His divine plan. This doctrine pervades the Word of God in both the Old and New Testaments. Somehow our churches too often save it for a Mother's Day special.

One superb showing of God's family portrait is inserted in Israel's ancient hymnbook, the Psalms. Ponder carefully:

> Unless the LORD builds the house,
> They labor in vain who build it;
> Unless the LORD guards the city,
> The watchman keeps awake in vain.
> It is vain for you to rise up early,
> To retire late,
> To eat the bread of painful labors;
> For He gives to His beloved even in his sleep.
>
> Behold, children are a gift of the LORD,
> The fruit of the womb is a reward.
> Like arrows in the hand of a warrior,
> So are the children of one's youth.
> How blessed is the man whose quiver is full of them;
> They shall not be ashamed,
> When they speak with their enemies in the gate.
>
> Psalm 127

The description begins with the foundation for the home. It starts with the *inception* and ends with the *impact* of the home. "Except the LORD build ..." The home begins with a philosophy, with a personal commitment. It is not saying you do not build your home—you do. Rather, it is a warning against the idiocy of trying to build your home alone. No way! You will never pull off the assignment as a Christian parent—as a partner in a dynamic relationship—without the Lord. You will never succeed even though you redouble your efforts by getting up earlier and staying up later. You will only ache, and there is no hurt comparable to the suffering of a failing parent. No amount of personal or professional success will compensate for parental bungling.

In this word picture of Psalm 127, God puts a blue ribbon on children. Look at His descriptive terms: He calls them a "heritage" or "gift." One authority says this word must be translated "assignment." Your children are God's assignment or commission, and He knows the very kind to send to you. Did you think God gave you children because of what you could do for them? That's only one part. He gave them because of what they could do for you. You can meet your children's particular needs and they can meet yours in a unique and special way.

GOD'S TROPHIES

The psalmic portrayal also calls children a "reward." Not a curse, not a tragedy, not an accident—they are the expression of God's favor. It is a thrilling sight to see your children through the lens of Scripture as His trophies.

Now we hear someone saying, "What happens to the couple who does not have children?" Though children are the obvious reward of the Lord upon a marriage, it does not follow that if you do not have children, He is not rewarding you. God has many creative means of rewarding His children.

If babies are born into your home, you are highly honored. But if, in the providence of God, you do not have children, then God has an altogether different and unique plan for you. You may discover the most distinctive ministry you have ever experienced in life—building into the lives of children whose parents couldn't care less. Some of us are here only because somebody else cared for us more than our parents did.

Children are also called "arrows." That presupposes that they are to be launched toward a target—and that you know what the target is. One major reason parents fail is that they have never sighted the target. Talk to the teens in the average church youth group about their parents. With many, you get a graphic replay of parental activity—often frenzied, directionless, reminiscent of the definition of a fanatic (one who redoubles his efforts after he has lost sight of his goal!). Good children don't emerge by accident; they are the fruit of careful cultivation. Make raising good children your clear-cut objective, the specific aim for which you are trusting God.

THE HOME-CHURCH PARTNERSHIP

Our concern for the home should be top priority, even though most mass media miss its importance, because the world turns on the home and church. Yet, neither one should eclipse the other.

A pastor friend once showed me his church bulletin with activities listed every night of the week. "Are you proud of that?" I asked him. He wasn't sure how to reply. *What if a family wants to build their home life?* I was thinking. When can they do that if they are committed every night to go to their church? The disturbing question is whether some churches are doing more to break up homes than to build them. Are churches engaged in a program of competition or cooperation? Do churches conceive of home as an adversary or an ally?

Many Christians spend time in parachurch groups. Two tests should be applied to any such group. First, does it emphasize the importance of the church? And second, does it exalt the significance of the home? In some cases the two are almost diametrically opposed. The home provides the church with "customers." A church should be primarily committed to training parents to do the work God has called them to do, not to doing their work for them. Likewise, the chief job of the home is to train family members to live fruitfully in home, church, and society.

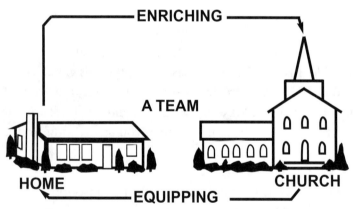

In 1 Timothy 3, God's personnel officer, the Holy Spirit, posts His requirements for applicants to the deacon and elder posts of the church. In both cases, very high on the list is that such a leader be one "who manages his own household well, keeping his children under control with all dignity" (1 Timothy 3:4). How can you rule the church if you can't rule your home? If you cannot serve well in a limited sphere,

don't enlarge it. If we are looking for a person qualified for leadership in the church, we are not to look at his public ministry only but also at the quality of management he brings to his home. If he cannot function in his home, then he has forfeited the privilege of leadership in the church.

On a flight from San Francisco to Chicago, I was seeking an opportunity to share my faith with a young business executive as we talked. He was returning home to his small corporation and the time seemed ripe to discuss spiritual things. But the moment I brought it up, he bristled.

"Would you mind if we changed the subject?" he asked curtly.

"Not at all," I replied. "But I'd be interested to know why."

"I'll tell you why I'm not interested in Christianity," he told me. "Christianity robbed me of my parents, and I'm not interested in anything that would do that." Then he told me of a father who

> *"I'll tell you why I'm not interested in Christianity,"* he told me.

traveled extensively as a Christian businessman giving his testimony, and of a mother who was busily engaged in teaching home Bible studies. He concluded with a touch of sarcasm and bitterness, "My parents were so busy leading everyone else to Christ that they lost their four boys, and there's not one of us who's interested. *Now* would you mind if we changed the subject?"

It was to prevent such a tragedy that Jeanne and I had made a deliberate, non-optional commitment in our own marriage: We agreed that prominence as a professor, or a writer, or a speaker, or even a homemaker would never supplant our roles as godly parents to our children. You don't think God ignores a commitment like that, do you?

Unfortunately, success in ministry is often used as an excuse for failure at home. One may spend more and more time at church where he or she is "making it," and less and less time at home where the family is unraveling. But God says that if we cannot conduct our home life well, we should not attempt to lead in a public ministry. Actually, we have nothing to say.

Simple math underscores the church-home ratio of influence. The typical child whose family is active in the local church may spend between three and six hours in church-related activities each week. Depending on the child's level of school or other extra-curricular activities, and assuming the typical child is awake approximately 100 hours each week, he or she likely spends fifty to sixty waking hours each week at home or with family. *Church influence: 3 to 6 percent of a child's time. Home influence: 50 to 60 percent.*

Columbia University once spent a quarter of a million dollars in research only to corroborate the truth of Scripture: that there is no second force in the life of a child compared with the impact of his home. The compelling crisis today is the need to train, equip, and encourage parents to do the job well.

Society Assaults the Family

Concern for the home is mandatory in the severe climate of contemporary society. Nobody lives in a vacuum. We breathe the air of a world that is sensual, secular, and incredibly unscrupulous. We cannot escape its contagion. It rubs off on us and on our children.

Look around. Magazines once devoted to clothing, cosmetics, and calories have now added moral decision-making with an underlying assumption of sexual promiscuity. Blatant suggestions for immoral living make up feature stories. Risqué pictures fill the pages. A recent issue of *Seventeen* featured a young teenager wearing very skimpy denim shorts, with the accompanying teaser: *No Self-Consciousness Allowed.* Twenty years ago the teaser read, "You can't tell about a man until you're in troubled waters with him." Today the waters are no longer described as troubled. Pregnancy without marriage is considered okay, in the name of first amendment rights. In some communities a baby out of wedlock is highly regarded, a badge of defiance against authority. Chapter 11, "Survival Training for the Sex Jungle," discusses this dilemma.

Ephesians 4–6 tells Christians to "walk circumspectly"— that is, look around, be aware of our world. We live in an era where the black hats win more often than the white hats. We must not put our heads piously in the sand and hope the nasties will go away.

Last spring two beautiful red cardinals came to our backyard. They mated, built a nest in a small pyracantha tree, and flourished in the quiet beauty of their secluded home. The female laid five eggs. We watched with fascination as she sat on them faithfully every day. But one day, as the mother took a quick break from the nest, a thief stole four eggs and disheveled the nest. We believe it was a squirrel searching for a meal. When we came out the back door, both cardinals were sitting on the fence very close to the gate, though they had been very distant previously. They were extremely agitated, chirping and chattering as if to sound an SOS or perhaps to scold us for their tragic dilemma. Their home was ruined and their family aborted.

What a picture of many Christian homes in which parents are preoccupied with other, "important" things, failing to realize the enemy is at hand!

Sometimes we tend to think of the "big problems" as outside the church, but unfortunately most social problems have infected the churches and the lives of church people. In our community a young girl in an evangelical church became pregnant. She attended youth group on Sunday night, and Monday she caught a plane for New York City. Tuesday she entered a hospital. Wednesday she aborted the baby. Thursday she was in convalescence. Friday she took the plane back to Dallas. Sunday she was back in the youth group—and no one knew she had been pregnant or that she had an abortion.

When the real issue was uncovered, the truth revealed that she had acted in complicity with her parents. Because her father served on the church board and her mother was quite busy with a church teaching ministry, the daughter was compelled to go out of state for the abortion, even though she was not convinced that abortion was the right thing to do.

A Christian home stands in bold relief to a pagan society.

At Dallas Seminary we have observed a steady increase in the number of students who come from non-Christian homes. Many of them are committed to Jesus Christ and love Him sincerely, but they struggle with built-in limitations. They sit across my desk and lament, "Prof, I can't get it all together."

Habit patterns grow out of felt needs; they are often compensation for unfocused thinking. A total absence of personal priorities commonly marks many of our present generation. Typically, they have for years scanned the pages of magazines with airbrushed photos of slouching entertainment stars and regarded them as role models. Even after trusting Christ, many struggle with images of their past immoral lifestyles. They have been brainwashed as youngsters and it has altered their perception of reality.

A physician recently explained to me that the normal lining of a healthy esophagus, the canal in our bodies through which food passes, can be radically altered by frequent acid reflux, becoming pre-cancerous and often malignant. Similarly, our children's minds can become calloused with the bitter backwash of today's moral filth. As parents, we must monitor the mental diets of our children.

Society Needs the Family

Although we care deeply about the upbringing of each individual child, our most vital concern for the home springs from the fact that it is the most dynamic means of perpetuating a dynamic faith in Jesus Christ. A Christian home stands in bold relief to a pagan society. Paul encouraged Timothy to "continue in the things you have learned and become convinced of" (2 Timothy 3:14). What things? The answer is in 2 Timothy 1:5: "the sincere faith within you, which first dwelt in your grandmother Lois, and your mother, Eunice." Timothy was a third-generation Christian. He was hand-picked by the apostle Paul to be his associate.

One of the most exciting things about working and ministering in this generation is to see the steady stream of young men and women who come to trust Christ and whose primary purpose and passion in life is to provide distinctively Christian homes for their children. Down through the years the greatest source of leadership in the evangelical church has been the Christian home. From generation to generation, the most stabilizing force in any society is the Christian home. The disappearance of such homes from today's scene is an alarming trend. It ought to stab us awake. It ought to commit us to the proposition that, indeed, the Lord must build the house. We'll never pull it off. There is no Plan B.

God has committed Himself to this.

Have you?

CHAPTER TWO

Marriage by Design

Husbands, love your wives, just as Christ
also loved the church ...
Ephesians 5:25

Good relationships: Everybody wants them, but where does one place an order? What Christian bookstore handles them? Are they available online? Do you need special training to qualify? Do we need to apply for a license? Or are good relationships inherited?

The fact is, many of us are not even sure what a good relationship is.

Our daughter Bev was in a freshman psychology class a thousand miles and two months away from home. The professor asserted that it is normal for children to reject their parents. "In fact," he said, "most of you kids would probably tell me that you hate your homes. There is a sense in which you should reject it all ... ."

Bev was out of breath and teary as she grabbed the first opportunity to phone home. "Mom? Dad? I'm just fine and I've got to tell you that I really love you, and I don't reject you. You probably think I'm crazy to be telling you this, but the prof said this morning that we are supposed to hate our homes and our parents. And I don't!"

How sad that the estrangement of parents and children has become so common that a professor calls it normative.

He even hinted that it is *proper* for the domestic train to be derailed, for the bearings to heat up, for the coupling to break.

Unfortunately, many young people—even Christians—have bought into the fiction that all their ills result from poor parenting and an inadequate home life. With professionals encouraging them to express their natural confusion about life, they develop deep resentment and often confront their parents without reason. The siren song of selfhood sounds so satisfying that they become convinced that running the old generation off onto the siding is necessary—if not noble. "Tell them to get lost; you can do without them," young people hear from an array of sources.

GOD'S SCRIPT FOR GETTING ALONG

In the opening chapters of the Bible God explains that He made Adam and Eve to be equal partners. After creating the man, He fashioned a woman and brought her to him as a "helper," a counterpart. Together they were to manage the earth and produce children. When they eventually disobeyed Him, God demonstrated mercy with coats of skin to cover their nakedness and with a third son, Seth, after Cain murdered Abel. When human failure occurred, God advised forgiveness, as when He told Cain to cool his anger (Genesis 4:6–7) and when He directed the angry Hagar to return to her mistress, Sarah (Genesis 16:7–9).

How can we break this vicious cycle?

The apostle Paul sums up the thought that is threaded throughout the Bible when he writes that we are to get rid of our negative feelings and to show kindness to one another (Ephesians 4:29–32).

Sociologists routinely confirm that children from troubled home backgrounds tend to make poor marriage partners, who in turn produce dysfunctional children and homes. Dr. Harold Voth, then senior psychiatrist at Menninger Foundation in Topeka, Kansas, wrote these dismaying words in the preface to *The Castrated Family* (Sheed, Andrews and McMeel, 1977): "The cycle of sick or weak people who are the product of sick or broken families keeps repeating itself, the effects spreading from one generation to the next, and slowly the sickness tears down the best tradition of mankind which made our society strong."

How can we break this vicious cycle? How does one convert bad to good? The book of Proverbs assures us, "love covers all transgressions" (Proverbs 10:12).

Where did the concept of love originate and why is it the antidote for dysfunctional families? The prophet Jeremiah declared to the people of Israel that God loved them with an everlasting love (Jeremiah 31:3). The apostle John expands on that core issue with his clear teaching that God is love, and that we love Him because He first loved us. "Beloved, let us love one another, for love is from God" (1 John 4:7–9).

Do you love God? "Of course," you reply. "Every Christian loves God." But if this is true, then the proof must come in our obedience to Him. John continues, "Anyone who does not practice righteousness is not a child of God; nor the one who does not love his brother" (1 John 3:10). And that is where the home begins: with a man and his wife, each love-related to God through His Son—the expression of God's love to man—and each related to the other in human love and mutual trust.

The strength of this God-Husband-Wife triangle is invincible. The closer each partner moves toward God, the closer he or she moves toward the other. Closeness brings into focus the other person, and knowing who God is helps us find out who we are.

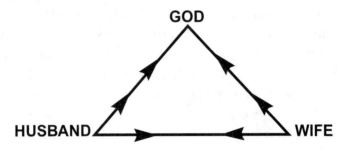

Perhaps this explains why God often has to back us into a corner or crisis, where we must focus on Him, before we can get ourselves as husbands and wives into perspective. A discernment of roles is absolutely indispensable for purposeful living, for marital efficiency, and for family functioning.

What roles? Sometimes they are almost lost in the pollution of mixed-up people, for we are living in a society in which marital roles are brutally blurred. In fact, many are convinced that there is no basic difference between man and woman except biological. With the advancement of science, these people say, even this will be thoroughly blended.

But here's a basic principle of God's design for successful marriages and families: Roles always determine relationships, and relationships create responsibility.

Ephesians tells us how to live a heavenly life in a hellish world. The first three chapters are the theological foundation and the last three are the experiential superstructure. Nestled in this intensely practical second section is a passage dealing with roles and relationships, and the responsibilities of husbands and wives (5:22–29). Notice two main strands: the husband's position and the husband's passion.

WHAT "HEADSHIP" IS *NOT*

The husband is described as the head of the home. That lends *authority* to the relationship. But the context here is extremely crucial, and missing the biblical context can lead to some unfortunate, contentious misunderstandings.

Verse 18 says, "And be not drunk with wine wherein is excess, but be filled with the Spirit." What does the filling of the Spirit produce? How will I know when I'm under the Spirit's control? That is not as hard to determine as some would have you believe. There are clear-cut distinguishable marks. The first proof-positive of Spirit control is that each spouse is functioning in his or her divinely designed role. Verse 21 really comprises the topic phrase: "Submitting yourselves one to another in the fear of God."

Some Christians contend that submission is the exclusive responsibility of the woman, but that's not the message here. God's Word tells us that *submission is the lifestyle of the Christian.* For wives the question really is, "Are you willing to submit yourself—not first of all to your husband, but to the Lord's plan for your marital relationship?" Don't let anybody fog you. If you cannot submit to your husband's leadership, your problem is not only with your husband; your problem is also with your Lord. You have not faced the basic issue of the lordship of Christ. The filling of the Holy Spirit always involves submission to Christ.

To build anything worthwhile, we often must blast before we can build. So in order to build a healthy, scriptural home life according to God's blueprint, let's first blast away some misguided concepts of what "headship" is all about.

1. Headship is not dictatorship.

A lot of frustrated drill sergeants are running around

God designed a functional distinction between husband and wife. To distort those functions is to devastate the relationship.

with biblical club in hand, shouting, "I'm the head of my home!" But you know they're not. If they were, they'd never have to tell you.

"The husband is the head of the wife *as Christ also is the head of the church"* (Ephesians 5:23). Elsewhere in the Bible Jesus is referred to as the "Bridegroom" and the church as His "bride." Men, we are to lead our homes just as Jesus Christ leads His church: lovingly, gently, faithfully, in a way pleasing to God. Christ does not cram anything down His bride's (the church's) throat, and neither should scripturally enlightened husbands. If we do, it is not only because we do not understand or embrace God's Word, but also because we feel the need to cover some unresolved personal issues.

2. Headship is not superiority.

The Word of God teaches that in Christ male and female do not exist. Galatians 3:28 says there is neither male nor female, bond nor free—all are one. Spiritually, male and female are equal in God's sight.

But being equal spiritually does not mean we have the same roles. In order for the marriage and the home to run smoothly, God designed a *functional* distinction between husband and wife. To distort those functions is to devastate the relationship.

This principle comes into full bloom in the life of Abraham and Sarah. Spiritually, they are equal. The apostle Paul's history lesson in Hebrews 11 states clearly that Sarah herself received strength ... because she judged Him faithful who had promised. Even unbelieving Sarah came to faith, and God equated her faith with Abraham's. *Spiritually*, Abraham and Sarah were equal. *Functionally*, Abraham was the load-bearing member of the team. God interviewed Abraham, not Sarah, to brief him on the divine itinerary for their lives. By God's design, Abraham functioned as the head of the home.

"But I would have you know that the head of every man is Christ; and the head of the woman is the man; and the head of Christ is God" (1 Corinthians 11:3, KJV). Jesus Christ had a God-given function on earth: He would be born of a woman, live, suffer, and die the ignominious death of a cross. In complete and loving obedience to His Father's will, Jesus submitted Himself to that plan. Does that mean that Christ is inferior to God? Absolutely not; to say so would be blasphemy. Likewise, it is heresy to say that to be in submission to your husband casts you into an inferior role.

Think it through carefully, wives. Your whole life rests on this issue. If you want God's blessing on your home, there is no alternate route. You must function by His design. I didn't invent it. The apostle Paul didn't dream it up, so don't charge him with having an anti-feminine bias! This is *God's* plan, and if you want God's blessing you will have to function by His specifications. You will never find fulfillment apart from it.

3. Headship is not being the exclusive decision-maker.

This comes out over and over in question-and-answer sessions. "You mean to tell me that if my husband is the head of our family he's going to make all the decisions?"

No husband in his right mind even attempts to make all decisions without delegation. May I remind you that Jesus Christ—think of it—Jesus Christ has delegated to the church the carrying out of His mission on earth. That's the confidence the Savior has in us! And that's the confidence a husband must place in his wife.

It is utterly ridiculous for me to make decisions in areas in which I am totally incompetent, but in which my wife is extremely gifted and capable. I am willing and eager to encourage her to make decisions in areas for which I have no expertise. But I am the one responsible under God for decisions made, whether I make them or she makes them.

4. Headship is not always being right.

Wherever we have people we have problems. A husband is not omniscient and will not always be right, but he is responsible for taking the lead in the home. Therefore, he is to be a pacesetter, a vision-caster who takes initiative. He is not passively acquiescent but actively participating in the decision-making process with his wife.

God holds us accountable for what He has commanded. Each of us will stand before the Lord to give account for how we have shouldered the functional responsibility He gave to each of us.

To the wife the command is submission, a military term denoting rank. She cannot be made to submit; she must do it voluntarily. When a wife understands that fitting in with her husband's plan benefits her by knitting their relationship closer together as they honor their vows before God, then she submits as unto the Lord and enjoys a win-win result.

Wives, let me issue a challenge: Are you making it easier or harder for your husband to function in his God-ordained role of responsibility? Women often say to me, "My husband just won't be a leader!" Really? Is it that he won't take the leadership, or that you won't yield it to him? In the face of stubborn resistance, are you willing to walk through a wobbly period of transition so that your husband can learn by doing? Are you willing to encourage, even insist and pray with him about leading?

HEADSHIP IS LEADING ... LOVINGLY

In Ephesians 5:25–29 the command is repeated twice: "Husbands, love your wives even as Christ also loved the church." The husband is to be the *head* of the home; he is also to be the *heart* of the home. It is his headship that provides authority; it is his heart that provides affection. One without the other always leads to distortion. The husband is to be a leader and he is to be a lover.

If the husband is a leader without being a lover, he is an autocrat. If he is a lover without being a leader, he is a sentimentalist. But if he exercises *leadership with love*, no woman in her right mind resists placing herself willingly under his headship, for he will love her as Christ loves the church. Christ's example for husbands is the loving leadership He provides to you and me.

> *"I have a problem. I love my wife too much."*

I remember one student who came to me and declared, "I have a problem. I love my wife too much."

I blinked. "Run that by again. I hear it so seldom." He repeated his declaration. I took him to the Ephesians passage, "Love your wife *as Christ also loved the church.*"

"Do you love her that much?" I asked.

"Oh, no, of course not!"

"Well, get with it!" I encouraged. Indeed, with the standard our Lord sets for us, even the world's most loving husbands have a long, long way to go.

Loving one's wife is a full-time assignment. It takes every ounce of creativity a man has to pour himself into this person God has brought into his life, "to love as Christ also loved the church and gave Himself for it" (Ephesians 5:25). Christ died for the church. He also allowed it to suffer in order to strengthen it. The present-day palaver about never hurting anyone you love is far from the truth. Love will always do what is best for the loved one. If your mate is willing to say, "Hon, we have a problem," I encourage you to get on your knees and thank God that you have someone who loves you enough to be concerned about your relationship.

"So ought men to love their wives as their own bodies" (Ephesians 5:28). Husbands, that's what God is holding you responsible for—to lead and to love your wife *as an extension of yourself.* Are you coming through for her in this way? Wives, that's what God is holding your husband responsible for—to be your leader, your lover. Are you making it easier or tougher for him to lead and love you?

CHAPTER THREE

The Great Staging Ground

*The home is the great staging ground for
the family's traffic with the world, as well as a fortress
against the world's intrusions.*
—Norman Corwin

That other little person came into our home—very subtly. At first there was no one else, just the two of us. Then all the indications pointed toward—something. The doctor called it a pregnancy. We called it a baby. Think of it—our baby! She was born warm and wiggly—hungry for food and attention. We shared eagerly. We cared deeply about everything she did. She never asked, "Who am I?" She knew she was ours, the object of our love, the living proof of our one-flesh relationship. And we taught her that God loves her even more than we do—much, much more.

Loved, wanted, cared for—most children in normal homes start out that way. What happens to fray and often break the bonds of kinship during the tattered teen years? Why does a parent so often resent the bold presence of his or her children a mere ten years or so after welcoming them so warmly into the world?

God's Word assumes that children are naturally to be loved and cared for. There are no long exhortations in Scripture about loving children, but the implications abound—like so many green plants adding vitality to the biblical decor (for examples, see 2 Timothy 3:15 and Titus 2:4).

When parents love God, they love each other and they love their children. Children naturally respond with love for parents and for each other. This love is the good relationship. This love is God's plan.

Listening far surpasses lecturing as a method of training.

Relating to children in the home as a parent is not only doing; it is also being. Like a diligent spider spinning a delicate web strand by strand, the parent must give of himself with singleness of purpose to produce strong rapport. In the process he also receives from the child so that mutual trust is established.

Helping Your Child Succeed

One wise man has said that while parents can create a favorable climate for children, only experiences consolidate the learning. What kind of experiences are you giving your children? Do they build or destroy the parent-child relationship? Let me offer some guidelines for helping your child learn to succeed in life.

• *Practice a sincere respect for your child's worth as an individual.* Does your child speak to you spontaneously? He or she will as long as you listen. Listening far surpasses lecturing as a method of training. If your child is hesitant to initiate conversation, it's likely that the OFF button was pushed somewhere in the past, perhaps as a result of a BE QUIET! or NOT NOW! response from you. When a parent has told a child to GO AWAY, either by words or by body language, he needs to restart the relationship with an apology and a focused time for warm, loving interaction.

• *Provide for your child's basic needs.* Don't make the common mistake of lavishing upon a child all he or she wants or all of your frustrated desires. Instead, focus on your child's real, basic needs: love, acceptance, privacy, a place to play and study, clean clothes, ownership of his own possessions, a sensible program of eating and exercise, and opportunities to make appropriate decisions. As each child grows, make money management a special family study. Always tell the child the truth.

• *Expose your child to real-life experiences.* Use births, marriage, deaths, and disasters as teaching tools. Encourage your child to ask questions and to express thoughts and feelings. By doing so, you will help to satisfy curiosity, allay irrational fears, and prepare your child for the realities of our world.

In her early years, Jeanne visited the site of a plane crash. As she viewed the wreckage scattered across a field, she was full of questions and her childish imagination ran rampant. An uncle explained to her in simple terms reasons that such tragedies occur. He talked about the importance of good pilot training, of obeying the laws of nature and navigation. It was a simple conversation but it served as a lifetime buffer for a little girl who might otherwise have been warped by the sight of the bloody horror.

Give realistic warnings about dangers. Help your child build a mental catalog of what to do in all kinds of crises. Through prayer, private talks, and by imparting a growing trust of God's Word, you can build a reservoir of strength, peace, and wisdom in your child.

• *Help your child to set spiritual goals by discussing possible objectives.* Many children make an early commitment to Jesus Christ in their Christian homes. Parents often comment favorably but then do little to help the child take the first steps as a disciple. It's important that we discuss what is involved in a decision to trust Christ, appropriate to our child's age, and help him or her set goals for spiritual growth by forming prayer habits; by studying and memorizing Scripture; and by regular practice of virtues such as helping others, giving to those less fortunate, and learning to articulate what he or she believes. In moving a child toward such goals, we must allow for failures and encourage, encourage, encourage!

• *Teach a child to handle life without undue frustration.* We may laugh at a girl who cannot park a car properly or at a boy who cannot cook his own meal. The man who cannot function without a woman to match his socks and ties is a frustrated individual who was never taught the basics.

Confidence grows in learning to perform well. A child should be taught to do as much by himself as he can handle. To build confidence, poise, and maintain safety, a child should be taught good manners and serious responsibilities. For example, the child who learns to interact courteously and respectfully with others has been given a useful lifetime tool.

Performance, however, must be maintained on your child's level. Don't expect more than he can possibly produce. Are you a dad who loses patience because your son did not score a basket? Or a mom who refuses to speak to her daughter because she arranged her hair unbecomingly? Such parental behavior pushes children toward just giving up.

• *Build fences for secure emotional development.* Set reasonable limits for your child's behavior. Just as surely as the backyard fence protects in a physical way, behavioral limits shield a young person from the fear of not knowing when to stop. The dangers of traffic, fire, drugs, plastic bags—all traps of childhood—can be greatly diminished if a parent deals preventively with calm, well-reasoned warnings. The same is true for the numerous, frequent temptations that are bound to come along as your child grows older. Train your child to keep cool and think before acting.

Things Never (Well, Hardly Ever) to Do with Your Children

• Don't compare siblings to one another. This is the first step toward bitter, discriminatory attitudes toward each other.

• Don't threaten. By doing so, you diminish your own authority.

• Don't bribe. Bargaining always makes you the loser.

• Don't lose your temper. This only reveals a clear lack of control.

• Don't refuse to explain. Your children will go elsewhere and leave you on the outside.

• Don't use sarcasm or embarrassment. These are the fastest ways to demolish a relationship.

• Don't dash their dreams. Doing so is your express ticket to the generation gap.

Threatening your children only diminishes your own authority.

If a child lives with criticism, she does not learn responsibility. She learns to condemn herself and to find fault with others. She learns to doubt her own judgment, to disparage her own ability, and to distrust the intentions of others. Above all, she learns to live with the continual expectation of impending doom.

Studies done with children who take drugs all come up with similar findings: extreme dissatisfaction with themselves and with others. School dropouts almost always report poor relationships with parents (especially fathers) and a paralyzing apathy—a complete lack of motivation.

There will be inevitable squabbling among children; that is human nature. But that is also the polishing process to prepare young people to mix and match in the adult world ahead. Parents need to distinguish superficial, normal sparks as young personalities touch live wires together from the deep, smoldering hatred that may burn out a relationship for life. Brothers and sisters need each other, but they are individuals in their own right and should be regarded as such.

When a child lives with parents who believe in him or her, that child will hold an inner self-respect and high regard for others. Everybody's sense of worth is enhanced.

Peel off the film that may be obscuring a higher view of your home. As Norman Corwin wrote in *The Reader's Digest,* "One child makes a home a course in liberal education for both himself and his parents; two children make it a private school; three or more make it a campus. ... All in all, the home is the great staging ground for the family's traffic with the world, as well as a fortress against the world's intrusions."

CHAPTER FOUR

Beyond the Nuclear Family

But if anyone does not provide for his own, and especially
those of his household, he has denied the faith,
and is worse than an unbeliever.
1 Timothy 5:8

The idealized Ward-and-June-Cleaver family structure of an earlier day has gone the way of the black-and-white television set. As though shepherding a family was not tough enough back when it was just Dad, Mom, brothers, and sisters, today's home often sees a single parent going it alone. In many other cases, the home is a melting pot of stepparents, stepchildren, adult children, grandparents, and often our children's children. The nuclear family of previous generations has become more and more rare as today's single-parent, blended, or extended-family homes gain dominance in our society. We'll look at parenting without a partner in the next chapter. In this chapter, let's address the blended and the extended family.

THE BLENDED FAMILY

In reality, every family is a blend, a combination of one-time strangers who moved into the orbit of friendship and eventually became members of a common household. The brittleness of families today, however, prompts frequent fractures. The consequence is a large number of rejoined family groups where stepparents and stepsiblings are called to accept, adjust to, and love one another.

Several years ago Jeanne and I were invited into such a home. Both parents had been married previously and had children; each had suffered through painful divorce and their seven children were all affected by feelings of rejection and apprehension. Yet as we met the children, who ranged from preschool- to college-age, we couldn't help noticing a remarkable team spirit and an upbeat optimism among them.

THE BYLAWS OF BLENDING

So remarkable was this experience that we asked the parents to share with us some of their secrets for blending families successfully. I have added some additional thoughts and called these secrets the Bylaws of Blending.

1. Plan the strategy of the merger. When two existent families come together, every member must be considered. Each relationship must be examined so that each cross-connection is understood and considered sympathetically. The new love between mother and father must be explained and gently extended with patience and acceptance.

2. Put a family agreement in writing. This document should account for each family member as a contributing part of the new team. Rights and responsibilities, limitations and rewards—every facet of home life that can be anticipated should be noted and signed by everyone.

3. Practice reevaluation. Daily routine tends to wear down good intentions. A regular family council is a good preventive for deteriorating attitudes. Each person should be encouraged to express his or her feelings; problems need to be discussed calmly and openly. Embarrassment and put-downs will not be allowed; all assets and liabilities must be shared. Obviously, leadership is required to make this happen and that job belongs to the parents.

4. Clarify authority and access to it. Families vary in their organization according to temperaments and abilities, but everyone needs to understand who is in charge and what to do with problems, criticism, and dissatisfaction. They all need to learn respect for one another and ways to resolve conflict, all in the process of learning the meaning of love.

5. Employ the tool of family worship. Nothing smooths relationships and nourishes a home more than a time of common adoration of God and prayer for needs which everyone shares. There is no greater stabilizer or healer of hurts. The warmth that is generated in loving God together prevents problems and supplies reassurance of a bonding that goes with an individual throughout life.

The idealized Ward-and-June-Cleaver family structure of an earlier day has gone the way of the black-and-white television set.

ADULT CHILDREN

Ever since sociology introduced the category of adolescence into our thinking about child development, the assumption of adult rights and privileges has blurred. The Puritan distinctions between children and adults in early America were probably less accurate, but they were clearly understood. Childhood turned into manhood and womanhood very quickly. Several reasons prompted this attitude, the first and most obvious was the critical need in Spartan colonial times for laborers and leaders in their limited life span.

Secondly, the ancient Hebrew traditions which formed the roots of the Judeo-Christian ethic of early America moved their children into adult responsibilities at early ages. Boys and girls learned basic rules of living from their mothers until about seven years of age, but then the boys began to spend time with their fathers as junior apprentices in their trades, and the girls spent time with their mothers learning the many tasks of homemaking. At approximately thirteen years, the boys were put under the tutelage of the elders and began rigorous memorization of the Torah. At a similar age girls worked full-time in home care and preparation for motherhood.

A third reason comes from the New Testament. The apostle Paul states clearly that when he became a man he "put away childish things" (1 Corinthians 13:11). This clear delineation served as a guiding principle.

We have made it extra-difficult for our children to grow up and take responsibility for themselves.

When child development specialists began to define the transition from childhood to adulthood as a separate period of growth, we, in effect, prolonged the privileges of childhood. As the American economy prospered during the nineteenth and twentieth centuries, along with a major shift from an agricultural to an urban society, citizens were relieved from the chores of rural life and families began to enjoy discretionary time and money.

Parents began to assume financial and emotional support for children extending through the second decade of life. Rites of passage, so mandatory in other cultures, faded from the American scene, prolonging childhood dependencies. In other words, we have made it extra-difficult for our children to grow up and take responsibility for themselves.

Not much literature is available on the subject of parenting adult children; therefore, families vary greatly in their adult relationships. Some families are extremely ingrown, with adult sons and daughters leaning on aged parents for support of all kinds. Others, with unresolved disagreements, break all ties and seek independent living, with no feeling of responsibility for their older family members. When the moral upheaval of the 1960s and '70s blasted conventional beliefs about institutional authority, the younger generation, by and large, adopted an attitude of privilege and protest against rules and regulations.

Most families with whom I have counseled in recent years have experienced some rupture of relationships with their adult children. Failure of parents to prepare children for a stormy adulthood and refusal of children to obey what may have been taught earlier has resulted in relational fractures in many American homes.

Another factor in family estrangement is the ready access to sophisticated technology, such as personal cell phones, television sets, and computers—all isolating children from the family group— combined with the dominance of the entertainment world. A strange and exotic distortion of real life exposes very young children to so-called "adult" viewing.

This premature imitation of grown-ups, often intensified by peer pressure from the community, becomes a caricature of real life and often propels the child into a lethal fantasy world. Many parents begin to "lose" their children trying to keep step with current fads.

Speaking to parents, Pastor David Wyrtzen wrote in *Raising Worldly-wise but Innocent Kids* (Moody Press, 1993):

> The entire book of Proverbs is an attempt to keep this young simpleton out of trouble. ... He thinks he knows more than his instructors and his arrogant

naivete leads him to the wrong place at the right time. ... this is the teenager who has nothing to do on a Friday night except cruise the streets. This unplanned "going out" is naïve. If we allow it to occur we are foolish.

IN-LAWS

One day, one of our children arrived home from college with an announcement: Wedding plans were in our future. The Hendricks family was going to have another member. One person made a decision but all of us were affected. True, this once-casual acquaintance had spent the night, eaten at our table, visited with us, and won our affections. But were we ready to make him part of the inner circle?

In-laws are intruders. They may or may not be truly welcome, but they come into a family with legal sanction. They are binding. Most often they are not pre-loved; we have to learn to appreciate them. They are essentially transplants from an alien culture, competitors for support and resources, a responsibility assigned without a vote. We Americans have always disliked taxation without representation.

As Christians we need to disarm ourselves and pursue loving détente. I'd like to suggest three disarmament strategies:

1. Preplanning. Warm, trusting relationships between parents and children tend to guide marriage choices toward those whom all will love.

2. Prayer. Sharing with a child from youngest years, in prayer times, expectations that God will bring His choice of a partner places marriage in the province of the Holy Spirit's direction.

3. Positive friendship. Families who build warm friendships with the in-laws reap bountiful harvests of mutual support and respect.

In-law relationships take time to settle in. The blending of two families tends to stir prejudice and bias. The most common areas of disagreement—grandchildren, possessions, decisions about a place of residence, money management, time together, treatment of illnesses, and religious preferences—need to be dealt with realistically and sensitively. As Dr. Joyce Brothers wrote in one of her columns (*Dallas Morning News*, November 30, 1986): "Usually when someone has difficulty adjusting to in-laws, it's because the person hasn't ever fully made the break with his or her own parents." There's a clue for parents: We need to prepare our children to leave us and give them the freedom to love a partner, fully assured that we will continue loving and supporting them. Our willingness to let go frees them in turn to maintain warm ties with home and parents. The real payoff comes as senior years approach. Grown children and grandchildren who truly respect and appreciate aging parents are the best social security we can have.

The Extended Family

The constellation of the family often includes satellite members. In addition to parents and children, grandparents, aunts, uncles, and cousins sometimes are part of day-to-day living. What is the proper role and relationship of this extended family?

A plaintive note is frequently sounded when relatives are discussed. "I'd really like to be closer with her, but we live in two different worlds."

How is it that two people who were possibly very close in earlier years can drift far apart? Proximity on the family tree has very little to do with the nearness one feels to relatives. Friendship must be nurtured, and the Christian especially has a responsibility to maintain a healthy relationship with members of his or her own family as a testimony to the power of Christ in one's daily life.

One woman complains: "We had a pretty serious squabble, my sister and I, twenty years ago, over a boyfriend. She married him; I left." A kinship that was once close tore apart and has remained fractured for years. Since then this woman has come to trust Christ. How does she mend a rift like that?

With eternal perspective, the irritations of life shrink to proper size.

Bridges can be built across the most troubled waters when Christ is the motivator. It may require an apology that you vowed you would never make. It may call for a humility of spirit that is beyond human effort. With eternal perspective, however, the irritations of life shrink to proper size. Paul reminds us, "I can do all things through Christ" (Philippians 4:13).

Even after twenty years, a birthday card with a simple inscription can be a bridge. *I think of you on this day every year (and lots in between). Just thought I'd let you know.*

Distance sometimes makes the mending easier. The hardest friendships to build are sometimes those under the same roof. Harder, yet in many ways easier. There are more opportunities. A moment to say, "Please forgive me. I'm really sorry about what happened." An opportunity to give: "Why don't you let me help you with that?" These are bridges, built beam by beam to cross an emotional ravine— to mend, heal, and love for Christ's sake.

A poignant picture is sketched in Israel's ancient history. The book of Ruth records the story of a young Moabite widow, Ruth, who left her family, her homeland, and her religious beliefs to devote herself to her beloved mother-in-law, Naomi. Naomi earned the love and the loyalty of Ruth.

Look closely at that relationship. Naomi achieved fulfillment in her later years by submerging her personal interests in deference to Ruth. She ordered her life in a pattern that helped the younger generation. She remained active and contributory and died a happy and satisfied woman.

Naomi stands as a worthy model for all mothers-in-law, so unselfishly opening her heart to her son's wife that a lifetime merger of love was cemented between them.

When a new family unit is established, its integrity must not be diluted by parental intrusion.

Two principles concerning roles and relationships apply to in-laws living with a family.

First, both the Old and New Testaments teach that aging parents are to be loved, supported, and cared for by their adult children (Exodus 20:12; Leviticus 20:9; implied in James 2:14–20). Paul wrote boldly to Timothy, "But if anyone does not provide for his own, and especially for those of his household, he has denied the faith, and is worse than an unbeliever" (1 Timothy 5:8).

Second, when a new family unit is established, its integrity must not be diluted by parental intrusion. Scripture says, "For this cause a man shall leave his father and mother, and shall cleave to his wife ..." (Matthew 19:5). If it becomes necessary for older parents to move into an established family unit of one of their children, they should not expect to resume parental control but should take a submerged role, in the spirit of Naomi.

With these principles to guide, it seems clear that when a family must decide how and where an older parent is to live, the father of that family must lead in making the decision. He has a scriptural mandate to see that his parents and the parents of his wife are cared for when the need arises. How? That depends on individual factors.

Ideally, a man and his wife should pray and discuss the situation before a decision is made. What is best for the individual? What is best for the family? This is a time to be coldly practical, yet warmly loving.

AGING PARENTS

Ever since Social Security deductions became a reality in American paychecks, retired and aging persons have been viewed through a curtain of dollar signs. Former generations settled their elder family members with relatives, accepting whatever contributions the old folks could make until they passed on.

Seniorhood can be very expensive, and with our average longevity growing with every decade, any ailing oldster who does not have sufficient private resources becomes the object of a cruel question: Can we afford you? Government aid is rapidly being depleted, and nearly every adult child faces the agonizing dilemma of what to do about dear old Mom and/or Dad.

Psalm 92:14 speaks of the righteous: "They will still bear fruit in their old age, and they will stay fresh and green" (NIV). Many seniors are doing just that, remaining active, having prepared well in advance for the inevitable weakness of their latter years. How should a family respond to grandparents?

Two important principles are threaded through the Bible. First, God sees mankind as His family, in a connected line. Age is secondary to family relationships. Second, life in human form is a privileged window of opportunity. God gives us a period of time to represent Him on earth, and as aging intensifies, so does a sense of urgency. Whatever must be done cannot be put off. King David declared, "Since my youth, O God, You have taught me and to this day I declare Your marvelous deeds. Even when I am old and gray, do not forsake me, O God, till I declare Your power to the next generation" (Psalm 71:17–18, NIV).

Over and over the theme persists: "… tell the generations to come the praises of the LORD" (Psalm 78:4; see 2–5). Aging is a family matter, and it is all about delivering a message. God decreed statutes for Jacob and established His law in Israel, commanding the forefathers to teach their children, so that the next generations would know them— even the children yet to be born—and they in turn would tell their children. The message must be delivered, and families need to help grandparents deliver it.

Our current culture has mislaid the purpose of grandparents.

Our current culture has mislaid the purpose of grandparents. Far more is needed than a pat on the head and the giving of a gift. Old people are reservoirs of knowledge and experience, gold waiting to be mined. No family should allow an older person to leave this earth before inviting him or her to enrich their family's lives by reflecting on their wealth of experience. How can we do that?

- Turn on the tape recorder (better yet, the camcorder) and ask questions: names of family members, poems memorized, memories of school, of church, of war and the Great Depression, places he or she lived.

- Dig out old snapshots and ask about them to trigger some recollections.
- Write down family recipes and practical how-tos.
- Talk about favorite keepsakes (Dad's old college plaques or Mom's favorite china or needlework). Ask about where they should go when the grandparent is no longer here.
- Go for a drive and focus on nature—glean what they know about trees, animals, birds, flowers, or geological formations.
- Sing or play music meaningful to them.
- Celebrate birthdays and anniversaries and take pictures.
- Teach basic computer skills so that e-mail correspondence becomes a pleasant reality.

Find out the individual needs of an older person and, as much as possible, allow him or her to be independent. Remember that privacy is a key emotional need. Being swept into the family circle for more than a short period of time is often humiliating to the aging parent and often resented by everyone else.

Well-being for grandparents also includes secure protection. In my city of Dallas, women over 60 years of age are most often the victims of burglaries, fraud, and purse-snatching. Be aware, also, that many elderly folks will never complain about lack of money because of pride and fear of embarrassment. Sound financial advice and a sensitivity to need is required.

Competent medical and dental attention need to be made available. Even our government's complex assistance programs for the elderly recognize this important need. Far too many elderly people languish in nursing homes, all but forgotten by their families. The biblical principle of caring, mercy, and respect should rule the Christian family.

Circumstances do not always turn out to be what we had hoped. Ill health, financial setbacks, loneliness, and rapid changes of modern life are often depressing to an aging person. Grandchildren are sometimes careless and unthinking, even if they are taught otherwise. Middle-aged parents often find themselves caught between two impossibilities. On the one hand youngsters are struggling in their own confusing worlds; on the other, aging parents are in need of assistance, respect, and purpose. Middle-aged parents can feel financially "sandwiched" by having to provide for growing children and aging parents at the same time. They may feel emotionally torn between their own children who cry, "Let me alone! I need some space!" and their aging parents who whine, "You're not going to forget about me, are you?"

At this point, the husband's leadership is needed. It may be difficult for a loving son or son-in-law to stand up and tell an older (and perhaps overbearing) mother or dad how it must be, but when the elderly become dependent on their adult children it's indeed role-reversal time. Sometimes a family council is necessary, especially when all live under the same roof or financial support is an issue.

God Knows What He's Doing

Domestic difficulties often stem from our insistence on looking at our home as an undeveloped negative. We see only the problems in big black blobs. But God designed the home for joy, satisfaction, and security—and He is the problem solver. When a home is bathed in the developing solution of God's true intentions, a pleasing picture results.

Do not overlook praying and planning together in order to prevent or smooth out misunderstandings.

Where but at home can you find a ready-made "fan club" where you are honored when you achieve?

Where but at home can you be loved for yourself alone—sans shoes, hairdo, and fancy wardrobe?

Where but at home can you talk about the little things that bother you and get a response that "tells it like it is"?

Where but in the family circle can you shed that specter of loneliness that sooner or later catches up with every unattached person?

God knew exactly what He was doing when He placed Adam in the garden and began home life. Home is the energy source. We all need to be plugged in, like so many appliances, in order to function properly in our individual worlds.

CHAPTER FIVE

Parenting Without a Partner

They that wait upon the LORD shall renew their strength;
they shall mount up with wings as eagles; they shall run, and
not be weary; and they shall walk, and not faint.
Isaiah 40:31, KJV

Of all the bruises that wound our American society, one of the most difficult is the plight of the single parent. A child who in formative years desperately needs a balanced mother-father home in which parenting responsibilities are shared is painfully disadvantaged when one parent is absent. The consequences can last a lifetime.

A *Newsweek* article, "Unmarried with Children" by Barbara Kantrowitz and Pat Winger (May 28, 2001), declared that children in single-parent homes are seven times more likely to live in poverty and seventeen times more likely to require welfare assistance at some point. These children tend to have greater emotional problems and discipline deficiencies, and have a tendency toward early pregnancies and family abuse. The formerly married parent who is deprived of a spouse through death or divorce also suffers.

Whatever the circumstances, a family missing a parent is like a stool with uneven legs, easily toppled. To encourage those who find themselves in this situation, let me share the following note I once received from a single mom:

> I'm a single parent and have been for five years now. When my husband left, I couldn't understand

why in the world God would allow this to happen. Then one day it hit me! Before, my daughter and I had a father in our house, now we have the Father in our "home." The Lord has given me the best five years of my life—so far! We really are a family now.

So it is indeed possible for the single-parent family not only to survive, but also to thrive! How can a lone adult cope with supporting and rearing one or more children and at the same time care for his or her adult needs for fulfillment? I'd like to suggest some chief concerns that must be addressed, and offer resolutions within a Christian context.

If you are a single parent, before you grapple with the needs of children you must settle issues related to your own disappointment and defeat. Guilt, grief, and anger must be confronted. If you are a believer, you have the inestimable privilege of the Holy Spirit dwelling within—God Himself, the Comforter and Teacher. I think it is absolutely necessary that you reserve a few minutes, ideally the first five minutes or more when you first wake up every morning, to commit the day to God and ask for guidance. Take this promise from God's Word and hold it close: "They that wait upon the LORD shall renew their strength; they shall mount up with wings as eagles; they shall run, and not be weary; and they shall walk, and not faint" (Isaiah 40:31, KJV).

Mental health professionals have long touted self-talk as a powerful tool to motivate people's actions. So just think how important it is for you, and the power of God that will be unleashed, when you meditate on the inspired words of the Bible! That can make all the difference between winning and losing in your situation. Ponder the meaning of verses such as Isaiah 41:10: "Do not fear, for I am with you; do not anxiously look about you, for I am your God. I will strengthen you, surely I will help you, surely I will uphold you with My righteous right hand." This, in effect, throws the switch that delivers energy and positive motivation. With God's help, it is possible for you to put down self-pity, deal with negative attitudes from your children, and face the challenges of a tough, workaday world.

SINGLE-PARENT ISSUES

Child Care

Every perceptive adult understands that children need capable and loving guardianship daily. Daycare is a key concern for many single parents. Obviously they cannot be in two places at once and often cannot afford to pay for the caliber of care they wish for their children.

It is indeed possible for the single-parent family not only to survive, but also to thrive!

In evaluating daycare options, much depends on the age of the children and their respective temperaments. What may be quite adequate care for one child may not work at all for another.

Custom-design your children's daily routines. Even tiny tots grasp the concept of being "a helper" when they know what to expect. It's important for you to teach the idea that "we are a team." Mommy (or Daddy) goes to work; the child goes to school or to so-and-so's house. Explain things honestly and simply. Try to walk each child through the routine in advance. Talk about standing in line, being responsible for clothing and personal needs, about being quiet during rest time. Above all, try to arrange some little surprise at the end of each day—something each child will anticipate that rewards cooperation.

Single parents of preschoolers often find that a combination of nursery school and home care works best because this combination offers variety and relief from a sometimes overbearing structure. Opportunities for local churches to develop creative ministries for young children are limitless, if Christians catch the vision.

It is important to evaluate safety factors and check referrals when arranging childcare. For example, note teacher-to-child ratios, familiarize yourself with food services, talk with other parents whose children are in daycare, and look carefully at costs. Once you select a daycare option, probably the most accurate barometer of its effectiveness will be the response of your child over a sustained period. Carefully observe what is happening to and for the child. Encourage him or her to talk and pray with you about the teacher, the other children, and other details of the day. Life-long impressions are being formed!

After-School Care

So-called "latchkey children" are among our nation's most neglected population. Preteen schoolchildren especially need constructive supervision. During these formative years, your goal is to help your child develop independence that does not include resentment and spite against you. Careful and sympathetic planning will prevent much heartache as your son or daughter matures.

Some children are amazingly capable at a young age, but rarely should they be home alone. If that is sometimes necessary, arrange for a trusted adult neighbor or family member to be on call to help out in a pinch. Other options?

Neighborhood YMCAs and other community groups often sponsor after-school activities. The wise parent will check out every possibility.

Aloneness and Depression
One of the significant monsters of single parenting is a sense of aloneness that can lead to depression.

Caring for growing children by yourself requires that you reinvent yourself. You will have to expand whatever resources you have in order to meet the needs of more people. Decisions and disappointments occur more frequently, and the constant bombardment against your lone self can become too heavy to bear. As a result, many single parents sag into chronic despair.

If you are newly widowed or divorced, it is likely that you will experience a numbness and grief that drags you through a tunnel of dark uncertainties. Occasionally there is time to prepare. Our son became a widower with three adolescent and preadolescent girls. His wife's illness lasted for a long time and her death was a foregone conclusion for several years before the Lord took her home. Wisely, these parents set out to prepare their children for the loss of their mother. When her death occurred, there was a minimum of stress because each daughter had been provided with a mental, emotional, and spiritual foundation on which to rest.

Loss is never easy, and death is a cruel mystery. But placing loss under the wings of an all-loving and sovereign God casts it in a different light. If you have been placed in a situation of loss, including the death of a spouse, it is important for you to acknowledge that you cannot understand many things and to agree that, on your own, you have no defenses against your fears. You simply need to throw yourself with abandon on the mercy of the gracious God. Ask humbly for His comforting presence and His adequate provision for your needs. Obey every command He has given, and—much to your amazement—you will find that all His promises are trustworthy. He is everything He said He is—the caring Father who tenderly cares for His children.

As a father and grandfather with many years of pastoral experience, I still found myself kneeling in complete meekness of spirit to see firsthand the heavenly compassion that truly transformed my son's motherless family into a healthy, functioning home.

But what if your children are struggling because their home life has been radically disturbed? What about the poor school performance, eating and sleeping disorders, aggressive behavior, blank stares, downcast faces, and/or self-destructive habits that may ensue after the loss of—or separation from—a parent?

All of these indicators, and many more, betray a deep-seated anger and confused self-concept in the minds of many children whose homes are deficient in meeting their needs. Unless these problems are quickly and appropriately addressed, troubled children may not do well in our competitive society. What can you do if you see such problems surfacing in your children?

There are no simplistic answers. In fact, you may need to work with school counselors, social workers, or other professionals to help your children receive the care they desperately need. Following are some general guidelines that have helped many single parents reach out to their children who are facing issues related to the loss of—or separation from—a parent.

Show sympathy. Talk to your children, but more importantly encourage them to share feelings, frustrations, and dreams. Don't avoid the big issues. Ask a trusted teacher or friend at church to try to engage him or her in positive, rewarding activities; despondency can be blunted by keeping busy. Never should a child be told "not to feel that way." Rather, the opposite should be offered: "It's okay that you're sad or lonely."

Then *guide each child into the rudiments of problem-solving.* Learning to be honest with oneself and to face circumstances realistically are the only viable ways to begin finding effective solutions to the internal turmoil the child is wrestling

> "Trusting God" is a difficult concept for a six-year-old child to grasp.

with. Help each child clarify the issue(s) he or she faces. Reinforce that God values and loves them and that He cares. Encourage the child to pray and to look for answers from the Bible, from you, and from godly teachers. Sometimes reading good books or playing a musical instrument will help a child cope. Art or crafts projects, sports, and recreational activities may provide healthy outlets. Memorizing Scripture works remarkably well for some children.

Be careful not to use too much abstract generalization with a hurting child. "Trusting God" is a difficult concept for a six-year-old child to grasp. The idea that "all things work together for good" is also hard to get a handle on. It is enough to assure your child that God cares, loves, and provides. One thing is sure: A child tends to imitate closely the true feelings of the parent—you!

Sometimes you may be tempted to explain in detail why a situation is as it is. Especially with divorce, analysis is useless and often only triggers contempt in young children. It is far better to reinforce acceptance and assurance of love. The important fact is, you and your children have each other … and you have God.

Absent Parent

When children are old enough to remember the parent who is gone, fantasies and intense yearning to reestablish the family unit can sometimes become problematic. Joint custody occasionally helps children accept their situation, but the wise parent will refrain from making derogatory remarks about a divorced spouse. If death has caused the void, it is easier to explain that God took Mommy or Daddy away. In either case, it takes years for children to resolve the absence of the parent. In the case of divorce, be sure to reinforce that the divorce was not your child's fault.

If you are divorced, it is extremely important that the parent who has primary custody not overrelate to a child and try to make a substitute mate out of him or her. Young minds simply cannot bear the emotional overload of a distraught parent who tries to find personal, adult companionship from within the young family. In her book *Parents and Children* (Victor, 1986) Dr. Grace Ketterman offers three warnings to a single parent:

1. Don't treat the child like a parent. Too much responsibility can hurt the child.

2. Don't use the child as messenger. If the child feels torn between loyalties, he will feel guilty if he does not take sides.

3. Don't let the child manipulate. Both parents need to discipline the child and teach her responsibility.

Suicide

The availability of lethal drugs and weapons has made self-destruction an unfortunate option for many despondent children. In recent studies suicide was found to be among the three leading causes of death among young people aged 15–24. Alienation, confusion, hopelessness, or feeling bullied, rejected, or insignificant among peers can drive a troubled young person to take desperate measures to call for help or make the hurt go away.

Relationships in your home are critically important. Feeling needed, appreciated, and unconditionally loved at home goes a long way toward helping a child cope with pressure, alienation, or bullying at school. If your child is troubled, encourage him or her to talk about it. Probe gently to uncover what lies beneath the surface and resist the urge to lecture or offer a quick fix to the problem. Demonstrate empathy and offer to pray together to trust God for strength, wisdom, and courage to stand strong during these tough times. Most importantly, pray daily—several times each day—for God's comfort, grace, and encouragement in your child's heart.

Local church involvement is more important to children during adolescent years than at any other age. For the single parent, such involvement is a "must." Attempted suicides are usually a call for help, and a competent youth counselor or youth group leader can be a great resource.

Part-time jobs, volunteer work, or other activities that develop responsibility, and thereby a sense of achievement, will tend to make your children want to keep going.

School Performance Motivation

If a child has lost a parent during early adolescence, feelings of security are already jumbled. The broken home often results in lowered performance at school. Many studies have shown how the typical effects of this situation—frequent moving and disruption of income—combine to threaten a child's upward educational mobility.

Deal with your child's fear. When worry nags, concentration on schoolwork simply cannot take place. Be factual and honestly assure your child that he or she is going to make it. When failure occurs, accept it and encourage another try. Resilience is a vital lesson in preparing for adulthood.

Resist the urge to lecture or offer a quick fix to the problem.

Deal with rebellion at its beginning. Signs of antagonism, which serve only as a mask for anger, must be vented. Athletics often provide a good outlet. Sometimes involvement in music or other extra-curricular activities can be offered as an incentive to keep a child's mind focused on the right things.

Immaturity

A child may occasionally revert to infantile behavior as a way of expressing disapproval over upsetting events at home. He or she may resort to hyperactivity or extreme apathy in an attempt to insist that things be returned to the way they used to be. During these times, if the parent can "keep cool," the phase will usually pass. But it should never be ignored. Steady love and a firm hand are needed on your part. Sometimes a wise third-party counselor able to explain Christian principles is helpful.

THE FAMILY THAT PRAYS TOGETHER ...

Family worship is the best unifier and ultimate problem-solver for any home. For years I have advocated it, but for the one-parent family this remedy is possibly the most beneficial.

With time usually at a premium, family worship never seems to be convenient. But if the parent can gather the family together before the Lord *at least* weekly, he or she will have built a solid and enduring spiritual base into the home. Children may be uncooperative at times, depending on the mood of the moment. But if they are required to be present without distraction in order to hear the parent pray, to listen to God's written Word, and be invited to participate with prayers and thoughts of their own, nothing else can be so satisfying to the deep spiritual thirst within them.

One central principle needs to pervade the home in which tragedy has struck: *God does not make mistakes.* Never has, never will. In 1 Corinthians 10:13, the apostle Paul reveals that God never allows us to face more than we can handle. He promises to strengthen, supply, and see us through. In Philippians 4:13 Paul affirms, "I can do all things through Him who strengthens me." God never promises that our lives will be easy. But He does promise to comfort, provide for, strengthen, and guide us as we trust and walk daily with Him.

As a single parent, you may sometimes feel as if you are hopping along on one foot; it's hard to stay balanced and easy to become overwhelmed. And it can be downright perplexing if the possibility of remarriage arises. However, you have a remarkable opportunity to be a hero to your kids—an unwilling hero perhaps, but one who can prove that you have "the right stuff" your home needs. Whenever you feel exhausted and overwhelmed by it all, hold tight to His promise: "They that wait upon the LORD shall renew their strength; they shall mount up with wings as eagles; they shall run, and not be weary; and they shall walk, and not faint" (Isaiah 40:31, KJV). With God's help, *you can do it!*

CHAPTER SIX

Building a Fire in the Rain

And you shall teach them [words from God] diligently to your sons and shall talk of them when you sit in your house and when you walk by the way and when you lie down and when you rise up ...
Deuteronomy 6:7

When young Joseph arrived in Egypt as a captive of the Ishmaelite traders, Potiphar purchased him. Soon the Lord began blessing Potiphar, the captain of the king's bodyguard and his chief executioner, for Joseph's sake. Eventually the Egyptian official gave Joseph complete administrative responsibility over everything he owned.

One day Potiphar's wife began making advances toward Joseph, who was quite handsome. She boldly suggested that he sleep with her. Joseph refused, saying that his master trusted him. Then he asserted, "How then could I do this great evil, and sin against God?" (Genesis 39:9).

But she continued to make advances day after day, even though Joseph refused to listen and stayed out of her way as much as possible. Let's read what happened next:

Then one day as he was in the house going about his work—as it happened, no one else was around at the time—she came and grabbed him by the sleeve demanding, "Sleep with me." He tore himself away, but as he did, his jacket slipped off and she was left holding it as he fled from the house. When she saw that she had his jacket, and that he had fled, she began screaming... "He tried to rape me, but when I screamed, he ran"... . When her husband came home that night, she told him her story... . Well, when her husband heard his wife's story, he was furious. He threw Joseph into prison (Genesis 39:11-17, 19-20; TLB).

Joseph was willing to forfeit his freedom in order to keep from compromising his convictions. What a powerful example for all of us!

In college I had a brilliant, gifted friend (I'll call her Julie, not her real name) who was unreservedly committed to Jesus Christ. In fact, she felt called to the mission field and upon graduation enrolled in nurses training to prepare for a ministry on foreign soil. Scarcely six months later, she dropped out of nurses training. She not only hit bottom, she broke clean through! By her own testimony, she will never go to the mission field and will never marry. She feels that she disqualified herself on moral grounds.

> *Joseph was willing to forfeit his freedom in order to keep from compromising his convictions.*

One day I asked her, "What happened?"

She said, "Howie, as you know, I came from what was called a 'good' Christian home. When I went to nurses training, I discovered it really *wasn't* that good. When the girls would say, 'C'mon, go along with us,' or 'How come you won't do this?' I just didn't have adequate answers. The only thing I could come up with was, 'Because my parents told me not to.' That wears thin!"

Julie's experience raises an important question: How can you communicate convictions to your children in such a way that those convictions become not simply secondhand (as with Julie) but your children's personal property (as with Joseph)?

There are two sides to convictions: negative and positive, the problems and the principles. I encourage you (and if you are married, invite your spouse) to sit down and think through your convictions in terms of what you want to hold to personally, and what you want to communicate to your children. Let me prime your thinking first with the problems you are up against.

THE PREVAILING ATTITUDE OF PASSIVITY

Many parents somehow hope for the best and plod along under the cliché, "We just trust the Lord"—which can be a pitiful copout. There's one truth you need to stake to the center of your theological thinking: In both the Old and New Testaments, faith, belief, and trust are *never* passive.

Faith that is genuine is always active. The psalmist puts it clearly: "Trust in the LORD, and do good" (Psalm 37:3). You see, your behavior either contradicts your beliefs or underscores their reality. Are you trusting the Lord for the means as well as the end? He works in both.

Look at the evidence. Noah sweated through years of preaching, of warning about the flood, of building a boat of radical design on dry land. There was no stagnation in his life. He was running a race against a global cloudburst. God said "Build!" so Noah built.

Abraham put his townhouse up for sale. To settle in the suburbs? Never! He toured the desert like a nomad. He spent a lifetime scouting real estate for his future family. God said "Move!" so Abraham kept moving.

Moses, plucked from the seclusion of the Nile River's bulrushes, became the favorite of the Egyptian palace. Later, the divine mandate from the burning bush shifted him into high gear. He defied Pharaoh, marched across the Red Sea, wandered through the wilderness, and never stopped until God took him from Mount Nebo.

These biblical heroes, and many more, pleased God because of their faith. The storms of unbelief were raging, but these stalwarts kept on building the fire of faithful spiritual fervency! There is no excuse for us to close our homes' shutters and huddle in the darkness, just "trusting the Lord." We need to move out to where the action is and mix it up with the society to whom God has called us to minister.

CONFUSING PRODUCT WITH PROCESS

We become dreadfully sensitive about the end product because that's what we always see most vividly. The end product is dramatized in a teenager who goes over the cliff, so to speak. You can see the wreckage right in front of your eyes, so it's not hard to discern the product. "Man, I never want that!" you say. But it's not so easy to become sensitized to the process. There is an itinerary, a procedure, a *modus operandi* that resulted in the end product you observed—such as the teenager's bad decisions that led to bad consequences.

Joseph made a critical—and correct—decision concerning Potiphar's wife. Where did he learn his instinctive response to temptation? No doubt many things influenced him, chiefly his commitment to God. But unfold the early days of Joseph's life and you will see him spending time with his father, Jacob. The godly patriarch undoubtedly had done his fatherly duty with Joseph, which Moses later commanded: "And you shall teach them [God's words] diligently to your sons and shall talk of them when you sit in your house and when you walk by the way and when you lie down and when you rise up" (Deuteronomy. 6:7).

No doubt Jacob had taught Joseph well. Before his jealous brothers ever threw him into the pit—the first stop on Joseph's long and difficult journey—the strapping youth had an indelible recording of godly convictions in his mind and heart. The most adverse circumstances never eroded his convictions.

In Search of Standards

What do you, as a single parent or as a couple, want for your child? You can achieve only that for which you aim. If you aim at nothing, you will hit it every time. You must have the target clearly in focus. Many parents have only a fuzzy idea of what they want to inculcate in their children. Three particular problems make the job even tougher.

Problem #1: Inconsistency

A particularly thorny aspect of parenting shows up in parents' lack of constancy and coherence with respect to children's perceptions of everyday living.

Our son used to come home from church, lamenting, "Dr. So-and-So [one of my colleagues] lets *his* kids do it." Later, I'd see my colleague on our campus and chide him, "Hey, you're a fine friend!" I'd tell him my story and he would roar, "That's interesting. Our son came home and asked why he couldn't do what the Hendricks' kids do." Together we would smile over their childish cunning.

Sadly, however, there are Christian homes in which compromise and dangerous concessions to harmful practices are tolerated. As dedicated parents, we must clarify the *what* and the *why* for our children because reality tells us that many professing Christians timidly conform to society's norms. For example, today there is virtually no difference in the divorce rate among church-going believers and that of non-Christians in secular society. The standard of Christian homes should not be what the community is doing, but the standards set by Jesus Christ. If you have to break with the accepted practices of the Christian community in order to conform to God, then do it. You will be sending a vital message on personal convictions to your children.

Problem #2: Biblical vs. Cultural Standards

To avoid confusion between Christian standards and the standards of Christians, tack a little label over these two designations that will help you identify them. Christian standards are always *biblical*. The standards of many Christians, on the other hand, tend to be *cultural*.

I'll never forget being involved in a discussion on a Christian college campus over the issue of hair length for young men. Everybody was so uptight it was unreal. Then the five of us who were talking glanced at the wall to see the pictures of the founders of the institution. And thus ended the discussion! You wouldn't believe how much spinach those men had on their heads. What happens in much Christian experience is that we get hung up over something that is culturally oriented and that a few years from now won't matter at all.

Some parents will make a federal case over several inches of hair. One Christian couple chased their son out of their home and told him never to return until he went to a barbershop. He never returned. They wish they had made a better decision. Oh, the agony that father has suffered. "That's the worst decision I ever made in my life," he said. He knows he acted in the energy of the flesh—certainly not in the power of the Spirit of God—when he sent his boy away.

Other parents (and pastors, and fellow Christians) may fret over children's attire, or pierced ears, lips, noses, eyebrows, or other so-called body art. Remember, cultural standards change over time. If you're going to take a stand, be sure you take a stand on the crucial (biblical) issues! *Your future standards will be different from your present parental convictions.* You have deep-seated convictions? So you think—now. *Give yourself ten years and a couple of teenagers, and what you think are convictions may become unfortunate prejudices.* And what you thought was relatively trivial suddenly becomes pivotal, absolutely central. Beware of being insensitive to the Spirit of God, because all of us are in the process of growing.

> We tend to react against the negatives of our parents while failing to reproduce the positives.

Problem #3: Reacting to Our Parents' "Failures"

Watch out for inconsistencies created because your standards are different from those of your own parents. There is inherent danger in this. You see, we tend to react against the negatives of our parents while failing to reproduce the positives. I once asked a student what turned him off about his parents. He gave me five things—very clearly thought through. "I don't want to produce *that* in my kids!"

"That's good," I agreed. "What *do* you want to produce

in your children that your parents produced in you?" At that point, his thinking was not as clear.

Perhaps you come from a non-Christian home. Yet even a pagan parent may have communicated significant things to you because he or she had convictions. Perhaps your parents had nothing to give from the spiritual realm, but they built values into your life that some Christian parents fail to build. Make sure you identify these factors. If you spent the bulk of your teen years dumping disapproval on your parents, you have a lot of hard, constructive thinking ahead. You have to get rid of the garbage and go back and determine what your parents did that was very good—and choose to reproduce those same things in your children.

HELPING YOUR CHILDREN "OWN" THEIR CONVICTIONS

Convictions, some people think, are like perfume. We dab some on the warm, pulsating areas of our lives and hope that our children will take in the fragrance, enjoy it, and profit by it. But convictions must be made the personal property of each individual child so that he or she can successfully navigate the moral dilemmas of the present and future. This transfer of ownership is so vital to your children's moral and relational health that I want to devote the rest of this chapter to exploring practical ways you can help make it happen.

Sharpen Your Personal Convictions

The apostle Paul writes, "Let each man be fully convinced in his own mind" (Romans 14:5). The apostle Peter tells us to always be ready to provide an answer (1 Peter 3:15). It is with such encouragement that we must share and live out our personal convictions with those whom we love.

My wife, Jeanne, tells how, as a young child, she had a

personal confrontation with the principle of honesty. She had been taught in her Christian home to be honest, but that was only secondhand truth until one day in a grocery store a clerk gave her too much change. She suffered the temptation, common to many, to keep the windfall and say nothing. *The store will never miss it,* she thought.

In that brief instant, Jeanne became aware that here was the focus of a principle. Right then, she made a decision: She vowed to be honest with money—with *everything*—from that moment on. Her decision required an act of her will; it has become a personal conviction. Now, when faced with such a decision, she knows what she's going to do *before* a question of honesty arises.

What Values Do You Want to Teach Your Children?

Let me encourage you to take pen and paper and invest the time *today* to write down some of the essential values that you definitely want to develop in your family. If you're married, do this exercise together. Here's a sample list to stimulate your thinking:

- Respect for authority.
- Selective friendships.
- Unconditional love.
- Mutual respect.
- Taking responsibility.
- Systematic giving to the Lord.
- Obedience to parents and to God's Word.
- A disciplined walk with the Lord.
- A positive self-image.
- A responsible use of time.
- Giving without expecting a return.
- Treating your body as the Lord's.

Looking over this suggested list, I am impressed with what it is going to take to put each item into action. For example, consider respect for authority. This is closely linked with obedience at home. If a child does not learn to obey in the home, he or she will be less inclined to obey the law, civil authority, or the Lord.

> *You want your child to become a giving person. How giving are you?*

You want your child to become a giving person. How giving are *you?* Do you always want your way? Whenever you make decisions as a couple, do you want your mate to always give in to you? The model you provide is the primary means for communicating convictions to your children.

Be Sure Relationships Precede Rules

Relationships are more important than rules because a good relationship with your children must always precede the meaningful enforcement of rules. A child is more inclined to accept your ideas and your philosophy if he or she accepts you. And the child tends to reject your ideas and philosophy when he or she rejects you. This is interesting to see in terms of a little diagram.

YOUR
CONVICTIONS

YOUR
RELATIONSHIPS
GOOD   POOR

Allow the straight line to represent your convictions. God gives you a child. All during childhood, for the most part, the child buys into your convictions—not that he or she doesn't question, but generally he or she conforms to your convictions. But then, inevitably, a child moving toward adolescence veers off.

What brings him or her back? The quality of your relationship. What your child thinks of you as a result of your ongoing relationship will tend to determine how far back he or she comes. The interesting thing is that most children who have a healthy relationship with their parents come back—not quite to the same place as their parents, but so close that for all practical purposes they are committed to the same basic values.

If you have a poor relationship with your teenager, he or she will tend to react and move farther away. The more pressure you put on, the farther out the teenager goes—an attempt to prove that he or she doesn't really need you. If you have a good relationship with a child, he or she never has to prove anything.

Let Love Be Supreme

Even if a child has received spiritual and moral teaching, if instruction is done without love he or she will tend to react rather than act.

Deprivations of loving discipline in childhood leave deep scars of pathological anxiety. I believe the lack of loving discipline in the home is a key factor in why many kids reared in Christian homes rebel so strongly. While their homes did not lack clear-cut moral teaching, the teaching took place in a context devoid of meaningful love in which the parent does that which is truly best for the child.

Love always acts in the child's best interests, even if the child does not understand that at that particular point in time. You should not be as interested in how your child feels and reacts now as much as how he or she will feel and react ten to fifteen years from now. True love treats the child now in light of the future. "Now" love should be alive with activity.

Writing in *The Reader's Digest* years ago, Norman Corwin provided a beautiful description of how love turns the ordinary components of home life into positive, life-shaping influences for our children:

> Of course a home without love is just cold real estate ... [But with love it] is a minuscule world. If it has ten books, it is partly a library; if three pictures, a little museum; if six tools, a repair shop; if one big, crowded closet of bric-a-brac, a warehouse. Whenever a piano or fiddle is in serious use, it is a part time conservatory. At mealtime grace, or in answering a child's question about God, it is a fraction of a church. In the throes of argument or the heat of discourse, it becomes a court; in sickness it is a field hospital; when you discover old forgotten letters, pictures, souvenirs in a trunk or attic, it is a wing of archaeology. When the kids climb trees, fences, high furniture, or other forbidden obstacles, it is a commando camp.

Listen and Answer

"The father to the children shall make known thy truth" (Isaiah 38:19, KJV). In order to explain our convictions, we must have communication, but sometimes the lines are frozen. On Thanksgiving Day, a young mother was seated in the den of her home with a group of friends and relatives. Her six-year-old daughter came in and whispered in her ear, "Mommy, I need to tell you something."

"Okay, Honey, tell me."

"I can't tell you here," the child whispered frantically.

"Oh, yes, you can, just say it out loud."

"No, Mommy, I can't."

And that was the end of the dialogue.

Three or four days later, the young woman heard (from a friend in whose home her daughter had visited) of an incident that had taken place involving moral implications. "Your daughter was pretty upset," the friend told her.

Later, when the woman asked her daughter why she hadn't told her about the incident, the little girl responded, "Mommy, I *tried* to, but you wouldn't listen, and Uncle Jack was sitting there, and I couldn't say it in front of him!" That mother learned a hard lesson—she lost a choice opportunity for communicating. "From here on out," she resolved, "when my child is ready to talk, I'm ready to listen."

Listening and answering. It's the communication line that's open at the vital moment. Moses knew about listening to and answering children. He counseled the Israelite parents, "In the years to come when your son asks you, 'What is the purpose of these laws which the Lord our God has given us?' you must tell him" (Deuteronomy 6:20-22, TLB).

Live Your Convictions Consistently

Our children subconsciously pattern their lives after role models in their environment.

Unfortunately, many children do not have adequate models, even among parents. They are not looking for perfect parents, but they are looking for honest parents. An honest, progressing parent is a highly infectious person. Your convictions are much more caught than taught. When a child watches you in the process of growth, he or she watches Jesus Christ being formed in you. That is a highly commendable thing to the child. Ask yourself, *What is there in my life that I cannot account for on any basis other than the supernatural?*

When a child sees parents behave in contradiction to what they say, the result is confusion. One writer likened it to a mathematical equation: A plus times a minus always results in a minus. In other words, what parents may say is totally erased by actions that do not support the words.

Christian parents need to be certain that what they say harmonizes with what they do.

Feed Your Children Responsibility

We don't become responsible people overnight; it requires a process. Feeding responsibility is risky. It means we have to allow children to do some things that we would probably rather do for them. We give them the privilege of exercising their own free will, and there will be some casualties along the way. Sometimes the children are going to fail.

My son Bill, a young boy at the time, attended a California camp while I was fulfilling a speaking engagement nearby. He came running to where we were staying and said, "I don't wanna stay there." We encouraged him to go back, but three times he returned, complaining. Each time we gently returned him with cheerful assurances, not wanting him to succumb to weakness.

The third time, however, we also asked his counselor if anything could be done. That's when we learned that Bill's cabin mates were making fun of his Texas accent. The camp director made some changes and the week ended successfully, with Bill wanting to stay when it came time to leave. He learned to accept the responsibility of being away from his parents, but he learned it little by little.

Constantly pushing our children beyond their comfort zones—gently forcing them to be responsible for themselves—builds their self-confidence. Responsibility is developed over a lifetime. Give your children the privilege of an early start so that when they step out of your home they have a background of living with their own decisions.

Sometimes the biggest hang-up of all is letting a child go. It stabs us. "He's going away," we sob. It's really not so big a hassle with the child as it is with the parents.

Houseclean Your Attitudes

Atmosphere and climate are paramount in communicating convictions. I would suggest that the most important thing you contribute to a child is to allow him or her the luxury of making a mistake. Let your child know he or she is free to fail.

Let your child know he or she is free to fail.

Do you refuse to look failure in the face? Do you overlook the benefits that are implicit in a mistake? Jesus Christ allowed His men to fail in order to learn. He let Peter sink into the water to train him to keep his eyes on Christ (Matthew 14:28–31). He allowed His disciples to fail in their attempt at casting out a demon to learn the weakness of the flesh (Matthew 17:14–21). Likewise, failure has a rightful place in the Christian home if it is used to learn an important practical or life lesson. It is sometimes necessary to lose minor skirmishes in order to win a lifetime struggle.

Be honest with your family about your own personal failures and the lessons you've learned as a result. It can be a great encouragement to children to know that Mom and Dad fail sometimes too.

On one occasion our family was discussing our witness for Christ. My wife related her failure to use several opportunities the Lord had given her to inquire into a young student's spiritual welfare. She had known him as a classmate and a debate team member, and she had flown on the same plane with him and chatted in the Los Angeles airport. She saw him again on a Honolulu-bound jet. The last time she saw him, he was reeling into a bar in Waikiki. Two months later, she learned that he had been killed in a train wreck in Africa during a trip around the world. She had talked with him at the beginning of the trip but never shared her faith. This sad failure was described to our children to emphasize the importance of seizing opportunities. It was, undoubtedly, an encouragement to them to know that their parents sometimes strike out too.

Seek God's Will, Not Your Own

Getting a child to conform to the will of the Lord is probably the ultimate goal of all Christian parents who have themselves experienced the pleasure, satisfaction, and fulfillment of living in God's will. Reiterate to your children, "It is not so important how you relate to us as how you relate to Christ." As our children have grown older, this has taken on new meaning for them.

When children are young, they follow their parents. Paul wrote, "Follow me as I follow Christ." You'll recall that our first principle was "Sharpen your personal convictions." Your children will imitate you at the beginning of the process that leads to imitation of Christ. All along the way, you must set the example of relating to Christ. This underscores the tremendous responsibility of parenthood concerning your own personal life.

We parents want our children to follow God, not a set of rules. Obviously small children imitate their parents, so our privilege is to personify God the Father to them. As maturity sets in and behavioral codes are internalized, the need for rules decreases.

We want our children to follow God, not a set of rules.

Let me illustrate. Let's say that you enroll in a computer course and are placed at an unfamiliar keyboard. The screen in front of you is blank, and you are expected to produce a printed page of material. You press a key marked ON. The screen lights up with step-by-step instructions on how to type out and print a paper. At first you follow every little step to the letter, but eventually you learn shortcuts to get from ON to PRINT. After awhile, you don't even look at the keys because you have learned the feel of the computer keyboard.

Similarly, our teaching of children should enable them to instinctively know right from wrong, to trust their own carefully honed judgment, and to go directly to the Lord and His Word for guidance. As they grow older, parental authority no longer awes them because they have learned that they have loving parents who trust a loving God and have taught them to have their own private time every day with Him. In other words, moms and dads have the privilege of teaching their children how to build a safe, warm, and dry inner self within the rain forest of their world.

It is not enough for a parent just to know something. In order to establish believable credentials, he or she must also be a person who merits the child's admiration. Children seem to be saying, not "What do you know?" but "Who are you, and what do you believe that I want to imitate?"

In his landmark study of teens, *Real Teens* (Regal, 2001), George Barna reports that, after researching fourteen sources of influence, parents were by far the most influential. More than three-fourths (78 percent) of the teenagers surveyed acknowledged that their parents have a lot of impact on their thoughts and deeds. No other person or group came close.

Inculcating Christian standards presents an unprecedented challenge to parents in the twenty-first century. Like building a fire in the rain, it requires know-how and persistence. But undergirding all is the critical need for prayer. If we lack wisdom—and we do—we have only to ask the Source of all wisdom (James 1:5–6). And when our Lord gives it to us, we must stand firm in willful determination because our children belong to Him and matter even more to Him than they do to us. We parents are stewards of precious gifts called children. This calls for an understanding of each child and of the nature of our hostile world. It demands a stubborn perseverance to keep fanning the sometimes flickering flames, to protect the hot coals. A warm and young life, glowing for Christ, is the most needed commodity in the damp, depressing chill of our world.

CHAPTER SEVEN

Are You on Your Child's Team or on His Back?

Humpty Dumpty sat on a wall;
Humpty Dumpty had a great fall.
All the king's horses and all the king's men
Couldn't put Humpty together again.

What a perceptive parable of our time! We are living in a generation in which everything that was nailed down is coming loose. The things that people once said could not happen are happening. And thoughtful, although often unregenerate, individuals are asking, "Where is the glue with which to reassemble the disintegrating and disarrayed parts?"

Nowhere is this disintegration more clearly seen than in the realm of authority. Whether governmental, societal, or parental, the discipline of respect for authority is on the decline.

It's an obvious fact that we are people of extremes, that we suffer from the peril of the pendulum. Too many parents verbally nail their children to the floor every time they squeak and make a federal case out of every misdemeanor. Other parents become overly permissive, paralyzed by their children's behavior, scared to death to punish and correct them for fear of permanently damaging their psyche. As silly as this sounds, many parents are almost saying, "If Junior decides to throw a brick through a plate-glass window, don't stop him. After all, you are likely to curb his genius for throwing bricks!"

But in the reality of home life and parent-child relationships, we need an authoritative base for making daily disciplinary decisions. Let's examine a slice of Scripture that sets forth a foundation.

DISCIPLINE—GOD'S WAY

The last three chapters of Ephesians are a patrol guide: how to walk by faith when there's a war on. Here Paul underscores a series of family relationships, and one is the relationship—or responsibility—of parents to their children.

Ephesians 6:4 states, "Fathers, do not provoke your children to anger, but bring them up in the discipline and instruction of the Lord." Mark it well; this command is addressed to fathers—not because discipline is Dad's exclusive role, but because it is his established (and exacting) responsibility. Gentlemen, you can never palm this off on your wife. If your children are not disciplined, that is your problem; God is holding you responsible.

Provoking children to anger is not God's way of parenting children.

This does not mean that the father is to do all the disciplining, as suggested by the frazzled exclamation, "You just wait until your father comes home!" Indeed, *discipline is a shared responsibility, but Dad is responsible* for all that is done or not done. As the head of the home, he is the one who will have to give an account of his father-home stewardship. He will never be able to assert, as Adam tried to do, "But Lord, it wasn't my fault! It was *her* fault!" (see Genesis 3:12).

The phrase, "Do not provoke your children to wrath" (Ephesians 6:4) is an intriguing expression in the original Greek text. It can be translated one of two ways. Either Paul is saying, "Stop provoking your children to anger," or he is saying, "Don't get [into] the habit of provoking your children." Either way, provoking children to anger is not God's way of parenting children. But what does this phrase mean? How does one provoke children to anger?

I believe we do this by either *overdisciplining* our kids or by *underdisciplining* them. Interestingly enough, both extremes produce the same results in children: insecurity, frustration, anger, and—when these three are acted out—rebellion.

Children need our corrective discipline. Is it essential? Absolutely.

Someone asked evangelist Grady Wilson, "Did your mother ever spank you?"

"Did she ever *spank* me?" he answered. "She had a strap in the kitchen that hung under the motto, I Need Thee Every Hour!"

That's corrective discipline.

Unfortunately, too many parents know only this form of discipline. I was riding in a police car one night when we picked up a kid who had been beaten unconscious by his father. The officer and I counted sixty-seven major welts on this boy's body. When we contacted his father, the first thing he wanted to assure us was that he was a disciplinarian. The sad truth is, he didn't know anything about discipline. There are too many people running around with a biblical two-by-four who really don't know what the Scriptures teach regarding discipline.

"Cut it out!" "Shut up!" "Stop it!" some parents scream. Their children are seven years old before they learn that their name is not Shut Up! It's amazing how much of this occurs in the name of Christian teaching. Often it is parents venting emotions in sinful, inappropriate ways.

We must remember the workable option Paul offers: "Bring them up in the *discipline* and *instruction* ... ." Just as every competent physician practices two forms of medicine—corrective and preventive—a good parent practices two forms of discipline: corrective and preventive. Unfortunately, too many of us define discipline only in its corrective aspect.

Corrective discipline always has a context. It is reinforced and made workable by *preventive* discipline. The effectiveness of corrective discipline is always determined by the relationship you build through preventive discipline. For example, I might ask, "Do you play with your child?" If you don't play with your child, I might answer that you have no right to provide corrective discipline.

"Oh," you might retort, "I'm the child's parent; I can do anything I want."

That's right, but you cannot guarantee the results. Your attempts at corrective discipline will have no foundation of preventive discipline from which to build correction, which will likely confuse, frustrate, and anger your child in the way Ephesians 6:4 describes.

Are you giving sermons at home, preaching without a license?

Do you listen to your child? (I did not ask if you talk to him or her; I know the answer to that!) When was the last time you threw yourself across your son's bed and said, "Tell me what happened today. I'd like to hear ... "—and then listened with genuine interest and empathy?

Do you spend quality time with your children? Do you know the joy of informal discussions with your teens? Perhaps you do sit on the floor with your kids —just talking and listening, captivated and involved. That's great! Or are you giving sermons at home, preaching without a license? "Listen up. Now it's time for Dad (or Mom) to talk!" You cannot program adolescents. You need to listen when they want to talk, and sometimes this means the wee hours of the morning. That may be the only time you get through to them.

Some parents are prone to get all shook up over a chapter like this. "Okay, Jimmy," a harried dad may say. "C'mon, we're gonna play. The book says I'm supposed to play with you. I don't have a lot of time. C'mon, let's go—get the ball." Dad then heaves the ball halfheartedly, his mind already on other things. What he is really telling his son is that there are one hundred other places he'd rather be than playing ball with his son, and he would prefer to be at any one of them.

How much better it would be if he said, "Hey, Buddy, I only have ten minutes, but there's nothing I'd rather do than spend it with you! What would you like to do? Play ball?" He goes outside and, after ten minutes fully engaged in joyful play with his son, looks at his watch and says, "Wow! That was the fastest ten minutes I spent today. We'll have to do this more often."

The curious truth is that children have more insight into this than we parents do. What really tears our children up is not that we don't have more time, but what we choose to do and where our attention is when we do have time.

Years ago, I was on the grass wrestling with my son Bill. My wife had dislodged us from the living room where it all began. (Jeanne is unusual—she doesn't appreciate a heated wrestling match in the living room. Imagine that!) Outside, Bill got me in a hold and I wanted to teach him how to break it. So I pivoted. Unfortunately, I got too much leverage and he went flying through the air like a missile. *Good night!* I thought. *He's going to have a concussion! They'll try me for child abuse!* I cringed inside.

But Bill bounced on the unyielding ground, then jumped up and squealed, "Boy, Dad, that was great! Do it again!"

Tough kid. But that same child would have dissolved in tears if I had spanked him lightly on the bottom. What's the difference? It's all a matter of relationship—relationship determines response. It's not the physical force but the personal friendship. Because of our relationship, little Bill possessed an invaluable assurance: *The dad who corrects me is also the dad who wrestles with me.* Do you gladly fix his bicycle tire or her doll house? Do you express authentic interest and participate in your child's hobbies and activities? Do you carve out parent-child times for hiking, camping, fishing, or innumerable other activities that will build the relationship bond?

Sure, discipline will be necessary. But your child will be far more likely to accept punishment and correction if you have already built a strong relationship with him or her.

ALWAYS NEVER MAKE THESE MISTAKES

When it comes to correcting our children, there are two words I am careful to avoid: "always" and "never." So let me suggest some things you ought to always never do.

Don't Compare One Child with Another

"Kimberly, why aren't you good, like Jennifer?" a parent may ask. One intelligent answer: "I'm not Jennifer." Besides, it's most unbiblical to teach your child to keep his or her eyes on another person.

Jeanne and I were blessed with four children. We never

cease to be amazed at how different they are, even though they are the products of the same home and the same parents. When they were younger, if I had asked a certain child, "Is that the best you can do?" he would have come right up and pushed ahead to outdo himself. But had I asked the same question of another child, it might have been the last time he would have tried.

We dads and moms tend to look for generic answers from parental pharmacists: What are the things you *always* do in every circumstance to *always* get good results? There is no such therapy. Perhaps that is why God gave most of us more than one child, so that we could see for ourselves the vast difference in individual children.

Never Humiliate a Child with Sarcasm or Ridicule

The male of our species is often a master with this needle. If so, he has possibly practiced on Mom. Coming into the house, he calls out, "Well, what burnt offering are we having for dinner tonight?" Or, commenting on his son's basketball game, he may say, "Why don't you try getting the ball in the basket once in awhile?" Sarcasm burns like sulfuric acid on human relationships, and it can leave especially deep, permanent scars on our children.

I have seen a child with a mild, occasional stutter develop a severe speech disability because his highly educated father and mother mimicked him every time he stuttered. They thought they could shame him into self-correction through cruel denigration. The long-term result is that this young boy grew to adulthood with a permanent handicap.

While it may be relatively easy to recognize the results of extreme parental sarcasm or ridicule, we are often unaware that even mild sarcasm or negativity can create uncorrectable patterns in children. Which brings us to the telling question: *Are you on your child's team or on his back?*

You can get off your child's back and on his team by trading in ridicule and sarcasm for positive affirmation. Wear your parenting badge with pride. If you look, you will indeed find something to compliment, thank, or encourage your son or daughter about *every day.* You can provide affirmation not only with positive remarks but also by attending games, science fairs, concerts, and other activities in which your child is involved and offering genuine praise for his or her effort. Be an active member of the PTA or other parent organizations at school. It takes more than words to say, "I am honored to be identified with you." Knowing that you are on his team, not on his back, will richly nourish the soil in which your child's self-esteem grows.

Avoid Using Threats and Bribes

Once I was invited to have dinner with a family where young Sally was served a plate with vegetables. Sally, about seven years of age, dawdled over her food and, of course, ignored the vegetables.

"Sally, eat your vegetables," said her mother firmly. After a few minutes, Mom's command became a plaintive request: "Sally, would you please eat all your food?" When Sally did not respond, her mother shouted, "Sally, I said eat those vegetables!" Little Sally stood her ground. Finally, with mournful exasperation, the mother whined, "Sally, please, *please* eat those vegetables, or you will not get any dessert."

Sally looked at me and winked. She knew the drill. Sure enough, after a little while her mother removed Sally's plate and brought a bowl of ice cream. Sally was a better student of her mother than her mother was of her. Instead of the clear biblical command, "Children, obey your parents," it was "Parents, obey your children."

Bribes may appear to work, but they appeal to the wrong motives. Let's say a father states, "Son, if you behave quietly in the restaurant I'll buy you a new video game." The child stifles his desire to misbehave—often only marginally—only in order to get the prize. How much better to say to the boy, "Restaurants are made for grown-up people, and you can practice your grown-up manners today. Would you like to do that?" If the child does not cooperate, then he should be removed from the scene. Nothing penalizes a naughty child more than being removed from his audience.

Nothing penalizes a naughty child more than being removed from his audience.

Many parents with whom I have counseled confess that they are afraid to carry out their threats. Afraid of what? Afraid that their children will turn against them? Afraid their children will feel unloved and run away? Happily, just the opposite is true. Children know when they are disobedient; they also know when they are loved. Parents who calmly insist upon good behavior, coupled with generous assurances of acceptance, will not fail.

We will seldom lose our children by doing the right thing that reinforces real love. Intelligent, scriptural love is always unconditional. You may not like what your child does, but you can always discipline with unconditional love no matter what his or her response may be.

TO SPANK OR NOT TO SPANK?

As child studies have progressed, people continue to disagree sharply concerning the physical punishment of a disobedient child. Many bitter adults tell of harsh discipline that drove them from their homes and estranged them from their parents or guardians. Many professionals, including some Christian counselors, strongly denounce any physical expression of discipline as child abuse.

On the other side are just as many professionals and parents who believe that corporal punishment is necessary for disciplinary effectiveness. Unfortunately, some of these parents, citing the motto, "Spare the rod and spoil the child," allow their anger (and wounded egos) to get the best of the situation as they whip their children ... sometimes unmercifully.

To spank or not to spank? What does the Bible say about physical discipline?

At least seven verses are included in the wisdom book of Proverbs. (See Proverbs 13:24; 19:18; 22:15; 23:13–14; 29:15,17.) Remember, the wisdom literature is not a list of rules but a set of principles. Drs. Walvoord and Zuck, in their *Bible Knowledge Commentary, Old Testament* (Victor, 1983) summarize the principle of these passages: "A loving parent inflicts temporary discomfort on his children (by spanking with a rod) to spare them the long-range disaster of an undisciplined life."

Walvoord and Zuck explain further as they examine Proverbs 29:15: "In Hebrew the rod of correction literally reads, 'the rod and correction.' Either the rod is the instrument of correction ... or both the rod and verbal correction are to be used."

Two emphases are important. First, any physical

punishment *that does not produce correction* simply destroys the purpose of the discipline and diminishes the parent-child relationship. Such punishment is simply counterproductive and should be discarded as an option for securing obedience. Second, the overall import of the book of Proverbs is its positive teaching laced with warnings about the consequences of unwise decisions. Fathers are told to teach their sons many important truths, but with a note of realism the book recognizes that sometimes sons will disobey or rebel. *In such cases, and as a last resort, a calm and controlled physical punishment may be necessary.*

Physical discipline should be the exception rather than the rule.

Please note that physical discipline is to be the exception rather than the rule. Most children, if they are properly instructed and consistently loved and encouraged, do not want to displease their parents. If and when a parent deems it necessary to administer physical punishment, he or she should always explain to the child first why this is necessary to ensure that the child understands the motives. Afterward, the parent should reinforce love and acceptance. Never, never should a parent physically injure a child.

Age is an important consideration as well. Until a child develops some ability to reason, spanking should not be used for correction. Instead, distractions and distancing are appropriate means for small children. When a child reaches age five or six, however, sterner methods may be necessary. Spanking loses its effectiveness when a child reaches adolescence, so parents should use punishments that are meaningful to the teen—such as loss of privileges for a given period of time. If protracted disobedience occurs during the adolescent years, a third party, such as an objective counselor, may be needed.

Afterward, the parent should reinforce love and acceptance.

Remember that you—the parent—are responsible for training your child. Proverbs 22:6 gives a clear command: "Train a child up in the way he should go." That directive means, literally "according to his way"—that is, the unique way in which God created your child. Thus, you must study the temperament and giftedness of your child in order to hold the line and guide him or her properly.

WHAT WILL YOUR GROWN CHILD THINK OF YOU?

If you love your child, you will provide discipline. If you do not discipline, you do not really love your child.

Neither can you evaluate discipline on the basis of what your immature child thinks of what you are doing. Your primary concern should not be what your child thinks of you now, but what he or she will think twenty years from now.

I'll never forget one student from New York who arrived at the seminary where I was teaching. Twenty-four years old, he had never once been away from his family for any period of time. His mother took him to college in New York every day and then picked him up. Then God called him to attend seminary in—of all places—Dallas. That's a long way from New York. So his mother bought him an American Airlines ticket, put him on an American Airlines plane, (may even have fastened his American Airlines seatbelt), and sent him to us.

When he arrived, he was the sickest puppy you've ever seen. "I'm homesick," he told me.

"I can appreciate that, my friend," I replied, "but it looks like you have a great laboratory in which to work this thing out—for four years."

He talked with various professors, and one of them was discussing this young man with me as I left on Friday for a weekend of ministry. "You'd better keep your eye on him," I said, "because I think he's going home." Monday morning I got the word—the young man had indeed left seminary. His mother had wired him the money for a return ticket. Doesn't that really seem sad? Later I learned that he was drafted into the army, and he *couldn't* go home! Probably the best thing that happened to him.

The point is, when you do something for your child that your child is capable of doing himself, you are building an emotional cripple. Thus, "training up" a child is far more than merely administering punishment for disobedience. It is the constant, continual process of preparing a child for the world by building within him the discipline to say no to compromise and to stay the course when life gets tough.

To help make that happen, let me suggest more hard-earned wisdom to help you discipline God's way.

Make Clear that You Expect Obedience

Some parents never expect their children to obey and thus are seldom disappointed. I recall the time I was studying in my home office as my young son played with a friend outside my window.

"Johnny!" the friend's mother called from down the street.

Little Johnny never flinched.

My son said, "Johnny, your mother's calling you." As if Johnny needed the information.

"Yeah, I know," Johnny said as he continued playing.

This went on for four or five times, and each time the decibel level rose considerably. Finally Johnny's mother exploded with a shrill scream, "Johnny!"

As calm as can be, Johnny said to my son, "Bill, I gotta go now." It seems Johnny had been down that road before and he knew exactly when his mother meant what she said.

I once visited the home of a fourteen-year-old delinquent boy. There was no bell to ring, so I knocked on the screen door and the boy responded. He recognized me and invited me to come in and sit down. Then he said, "I bet you're thirsty, aren't you, Mister?" It was a hot day, and I was. "I'll go get you some water." He disappeared into the kitchen and came back with a peanut butter jar, not too well washed, filled with water.

Just about the time he got to me, his mother appeared in the doorway. "Get outa here!" she screamed at her son, and he dumped the whole thing right down the front of me. I have rarely heard a woman—or a man—curse as she did.

Finally she snarled, "That kid can't do anything right!"

"You know, Lady," I replied, "I hate to start this interview on a negative note, but I couldn't disagree with you more. I'm proud of your boy."

"Whad'ya mean, you're proud of him? Look at what he did to you."

"Did you ever make a mistake?" I asked. "To be perfectly honest, if you had shouted at me the way you did at him, I'd have spilled that water too."

"He can't do anything right," she repeated.

"Lady, as long as you continue to say 'he can't,' he won't."

Do you ever tell your child he or she "can't"? Doing that provides the basic building block for the shaky structure of inferiority feelings. One of my primary tasks as a professor at the seminary was to reach out to students who perhaps for the first time had found somebody who believed in them. I hope, by God's grace, that you believe in your child and that you impart your belief that he or she truly wants to do well and right.

Don't Be Afraid to Admit Your Own Mistakes

One day after a long day of teaching at the seminary, I arrived home around eight o'clock only to encounter a clear case of attempted homicide. My two boys were at it again. So I moved into action and disciplined the older boy, who was obviously the aggressor. Later, as I went into the bedroom, my lovely wife said, "Sweetheart, you missed."

"How's that?"

"Let me tell you what happened *before* you arrived."

Of course, her explanation completely changed the picture, and I had to do what I think is difficult for any parent—apologize. I went into the kitchen where the older boy, still sobbing, had been assigned to the dishpan. I said, "Bob, I'm very sorry. I acted too soon. I goofed. I didn't have all the facts."

"Sure, Dad, that's okay. We all make mistakes." We sure do. Even seminary professors!

I'll never forget him putting his arm around me and saying, "Sure, Dad, that's okay. We all make mistakes."

We sure do. Even seminary professors! Your child does not expect you to be a perfect parent, but he or she does expect you to be an honest one who is secure enough to say, "I'm sorry. I made a mistake."

Allow the Child to Express His or Her Viewpoint

When our children were quite small, my students asked me to make a tape of one of our family councils. We happened to be discussing the problem of tidiness. I realize this is not a hassle for every home, but there were times when our home seemed to resemble a tornado alley. During the course of the discussion, my children were all confessing the sins of their sister, Beverly, who was about four years old.

Then little Bev jarred the symposium with this broadside: "But Daddy, you didn't lower it!"

Do you know what she was talking about? Do you have closets in your home? Check out how high the clothes rod is—especially from the perspective of a four-year-old child. I had promised her, "Honey, one of these days Daddy will lower it so you can hang up your clothes." But I had not done so.

You see, we were expecting a four year old to do something that was absolutely impossible for her to do. Furthermore, I had made no provision to help.

Recognize the Difference Between Childishness and Rebellion

Much parental discipline is arbitrary and without value because it presupposes a maturity that children do not possess. There is an important distinction between childishness and rebellion. Don't confuse them.

A Dallas woman, mother of three girls, shared a quotation with one of my classes that impressed me as being loaded with realism. Struck by the sobering responsibility of having a teenager, she told her oldest daughter, "Darling, I just want you to know I've never been down this road before. You're the first teen I've ever had, and I'm sure I'm going to make some mistakes. But I want you to know that I love you, and everything I do will be because I love you. If I discover I'm wrong, I'll be the first one to tell you."

You'll never get a negative reaction using an approach like that.

Provide the Freedom to Learn through Mistakes

When Jeanne and I were married, we were given a lovely set of pottery. In time our children arrived, and we faced a critical decision. *Will we keep the dishes intact and have children who do not know how to wash and dry dishes? Or will we train the children to do the dishes and perhaps, in the process, lose a few?* If you want to know which route we took, you should see the one remaining remnant in our china closet.

Allow your children the luxury of a few mistakes. Far worse than a broken china dish is a child who becomes afraid to try new things or tackle responsibilities because he's learned that innocent mistakes will be prosecuted. You may have to sacrifice a few material treasures to the more-important process of teaching responsibility to your children. It's a worthwhile tradeoff.

When I was a boy, I loved to play checkers. In fact, I considered myself to be something of a champion checker player. There was an elderly gentleman in the community who was purported to be the best, but in my naïveté I felt there was only one reason he had that reputation: He had never played me.

Allow your children the luxury of a few mistakes.

One day I was hanging around where he played and to my surprise, he said, "Son, how would you like to play checkers?" Before he finished getting the words out, I was busy setting up the checkers on the board. We exchanged a few moves, and then he fed me a checker and said, "Jump me." And then another, and another. I thought, *This is easier than I expected!*

As if it were yesterday, I can still remember the puff of his pipe and the wry smile that broke out on his lips as I watched him take a checker and move through my men to the other side. "King me!" He had wiped every one of my checkers off the board with one king, and I got a liberal arts education in checkers. No good checker player minds losing a few checkers as long as he's headed for king territory.

Did you, as a parent, lose a few checkers this week? The question is, where are you headed? King territory? Do you view your children as problems or as potential? Do you view them in terms of *what they are* or in terms of *what they are to become* by the power of God working within them—and in you?

CHAPTER EIGHT

Your Home-to-Heaven Hotline

"Do not hinder them from coming to Me;
for the kingdom of heaven belongs to such as these."
Matthew 19:14

One of the most remarkable revelations of God to be found in His Word is that which portrays Him as the "seeking God."

Jesus proclaimed in Luke 19:10, for example, that "the Son of Man has come to seek and to save that which was lost." God in quest of souls to save—that is the genius of the gospel. *And it is why Christianity is not a religion.* All religions have one thing in common: They are man's search for God. Christianity, on the other hand, is a revelation—of God's search for man. It was God who came walking in the cool of the garden asking, "Adam, where are you?"

John 4 reveals something amazing about the seeking God through the record of our Savior's encounter with the woman of Samaria. She sought to embroil Him in a discussion concerning the location of worship, but our Lord put His finger on the real issue: "You worship that which you do not know; we worship that which we know, for salvation is from the Jews. But an hour is coming, and now is, when the true worshipers shall worship the Father in spirit and truth; for such people the Father seeks to be His worshipers" (John 4:22-23).

Don't ask me to explain that last phrase; I can't. I'm only thankful to God that I can *experience* it. I've never recovered from the impact of this truth that God is seeking *my* worship. We grieve the Holy Spirit when we spurn that which He seeks.

One day a student came into my office and said, "Prof, I'm not getting very much out of my quiet time."

I'm sure I jarred him no end when I replied, "My friend, did it ever occur to you that it really makes very little difference what you get out of it? The important thing is what God gets out of it. God is seeking your worship."

Worship Is Not Optional

To the believer, worship is not a luxury; it is life. It's not optional; it's essential. It's not something reserved for a body of individuals who might engage in it if and when they have the time or the feeling is right. Nor is it to be limited to a progression of praise-and-Scripture music sung with devotion and emotion.

Family prayer times are vital to acquiring heaven's help in your home.

Worship is a personal response to divine revelation and, as such, it is the Christian's highest occupation. God has revealed Himself, and it is up to us to respond. But, alas, worship is the lost chord of evangelicalism. Despite an obvious increase in "worship time" (i.e. contemporary praise and prayer music) enjoyed in most church services, the act of unscripted, deeply personal worship is largely missing in our churches. But worse—and probably the reason it's missing in church—is the fact that worship is absent in most Christian homes as well.

Family prayer and worship times are vital to acquiring heaven's help in your home. Today more than ever, parents and children need to gather for frequent, unhurried times of gratitude for God's blessings, prayer for one another, and reading and discussion of the Word. Today more than ever, families need the inner strength, assurance, and calm that comes from uniting in prayer before the heavenly Father to praise His name and cast our burdens on Him.

Today more than ever, we need to take full advantage of the wonderful "home-to-heaven hotline" God has provided as we wrestle with the challenges of parenthood and of real life in a frightening world.

EXCUSES, EXCUSES

But too few of us are using that hotline. Why? Let's examine the excuses we often give for not engaging in the joy of family worship.

"I Don't Have Time!"

Finding time for family worship is a matter of priorities. You don't have time for what? To do that which God is seeking?

When I was pastoring in the city of Fort Worth, Texas, a father of five had become remiss in his attendance at Sunday worship services—and by all indications, extremely delinquent as a father and in his walk with God. Concerned, I paid a pastoral call to confront him with his defection. During the course of our conversation, he said, "Pastor, you don't understand. I don't have time. I have to work."

"Who said you had to work?" I asked.

"It's obvious," he replied. "If you don't work, you don't eat."

"Who said you had to eat?"

"Oh, c'mon, Pastor. Be realistic. If you don't eat, you don't live!"

"Who said you have to live?" I asked. "Give me one verse of Scripture that says you have to live. Did it ever occur to you that it would be better for you to die in fellowship with Jesus Christ than to go on living outside of fellowship with Him?"

"I never thought of it that way," he said.

I hadn't either, but I didn't tell him that! But here's the issue: How high on your priority list is fellowship with the infinite God? I'm not talking just about fellowship with others in church, though that is very important to the Christian family. I'm talking about personal time in which it's just you and God walking and talking together, your heart pure before Him, enjoying each other's presence?

Mark 1:35 is an insightful verse of Scripture: "And in the early morning while it was still dark, He [Jesus] arose and went out and departed to a lonely place, and was praying there." Which morning? Why, the morning after the busiest recorded day in Jesus' life. Only fifty-two days of His life on earth are recorded in the Gospels. The earlier part of this chapter records a busy day crowded with miracles, teaching, and exposure to large throngs of people. Only someone who has been before large groups of people can appreciate the physical and emotional drain of such a day. Don't you think Jesus had earned the right to sleep in the following morning? Of course! But the morning after that busy day, Jesus didn't sleep in—nor did He jump right back into His work. Instead, He rose before dawn to enjoy fellowship with His Father. That's how high worship was on His priority list.

Have you learned anything about the barrenness of busyness? We live in a culture that keeps most of us running from the moment our feet hit the floor in the morning until we lift them into our blankets late at night. There can be a sterility to activity. Much of it is nothing more than an anesthetic to deaden the pain of an empty life. But we do not have to run on empty. Indeed, we can choose whether to run with the rush or, in healthy contrast, reorder and live by thoughtful priorities that fill us with God's strength to live each day more effectively.

"It's Not Convenient!"

The average person is looking for a religion that is comfortable and convenient. And there are plenty of them on the market. But we cannot take cost and conflict out of Christianity and still have the genuine item.

I can say emphatically from experience that if you are looking for a convenient time to have family worship, forget it. It will never be easy. In fact, I am convinced that the devil will unleash everything in his arsenal to bomb away your family worship—anything to keep you from fellowship with the Father.

There is a price tag to worshiping the living God. Second Samuel 24:24 gives us a glimpse into David's commitment to personal worship: "I will not offer burnt offerings to the Lord my God which cost me nothing." It costs you nothing to accept the gift of God, which is eternal life. But it may cost you everything to have a spiritual life that has virility and impact.

"Watch over your heart with all diligence," warns Proverbs 4:23, "for from it flow the springs of life." The Christian life is a discipline, not a dream.

"I Don't Know How!"

The matter of technique is probably the most legitimate

problem Christians have regarding personal and family worship. Maybe you have no model because you didn't come from a Christian home. This was my problem. When I recognized my responsibility in this critical area of family life, I was like a babe in the woods.

Some years ago I was ministering at a Christian conference center and in the course of a message mentioned the "family altar." At the end of the session, a lady came forward and asked, "About that family altar, do they handle them here in the bookstore?" When I discovered she was from a Catholic background, I understood immediately what she was asking. A person can go to a Roman Catholic bookstore, buy a little set of equipment, and be in business. Now that she had become an evangelical, she thought there must be a similar set of equipment.

I sympathized with this woman because I find that those of us in the preaching and teaching fields are often long on exhortation but short on explanation. We constantly tell people *what* they ought to do but we don't often bother to tell them *how* to do it. (We'll discuss the *how* in a moment.)

"We Really Don't Need It!"

A man said to me, "You're going overboard on this family worship thing. Isn't it enough to go to church on Sunday?" This is compartmentalized Christianity—going through the little religious routine on Sunday and placing the Lord on call the rest of the week in case of trouble.

But the Bible says, "Whatever you do in word or deed, do all in the name of the Lord Jesus, giving thanks through Him to God the Father" (Colossians 3:17). Christianity affects all of life. It revolutionizes the whole of human experience.

Excuses evaporate upon examination. There's quite a difference between a good, sound reason and a reason that sounds good. If you want to have family worship, you will find a way. If you don't, you will find an excuse.

As a parent, it's your call. Which will it be? Which choice is best for your home?

Talk to God Together

Family worship should include a time when you talk with God. Early in our own family life, we used a loose-leaf notebook. On one side we wrote We Ask and on the other side *He Answers.* I wouldn't trade for anything what this taught my children about the theology of prayer. There is nothing quite as instructive to a child as writing down something specific for which he or she asks God and then, as God responds to the child's faith, experiencing the excitement and enthusiasm—and instruction—of writing *Yes* on the answer side of the page.

Of course there were times when we had to write *No.* Have you reminisced about unwise requests you have made of God? If He replied *No,* there's a lesson for all of us. A good father does not grant every wish. He gives only what is best.

Timing is often very important. Sometimes God answers prayer with *Wait*—not because He isn't ready but often because we are not ready.

God wants us to pray about everything. Everything excludes nothing. I hope it doesn't disturb you when your children pray about the bicycle, the dog, the fence, the sand pile, and all the other realities in their young lives. When our children were young, a scholarly man visited our home. The reason I know he was scholarly is that he told me so—three times! He participated in our time of family worship. In typical style, our children prayed about the fence and thanked the Lord for the tricycle.

I could tell this was rotting our guest's theological socks. Afterward he took me aside and said, "Professor Hendricks, you don't mean to tell me you teach at a theological seminary and you encourage your children to pray about things like that."

God wants us to pray about every-thing. Everything excludes nothing.

"Certainly!" I exclaimed. "Do you ever pray for your Ford?" I knew he did; he was riding mostly on faith and fabric.

"Oh, yes, of course."

"What ever made you think your Ford is more important to God than a little boy's tricycle?" Then I added, "Do you ever pray for protection?"

"Of course. I never get into my car without praying about the hazards of the highway."

"Well," I explained, "protection is what my daughter is praying for when she thanks Jesus for the fence that keeps out those great, big dogs."

The problem of becoming "learned adults" is that we often get educated beyond our intelligence. A child needs to pray at the level of his or her own understanding and needs. Jesus understands. In fact, He takes such delight in a child's fellowship that He rebuked His disciples, "... do not hinder them [the little children gathered around Jesus] from coming to Me; for the kingdom of heaven belongs to such as these" (Matthew 19:14).

God's home-to-heaven hotline is open to men, women, boys, and girls of all ages. And He's listening.

LISTEN TO GOD TOGETHER

Through prayer, we talk to God. Through the Bible, God talks to us.

One guideline is paramount in personal or family time with God: Don't multiply Scripture; make it meaningful. There is nothing magical about reading 417 verses in one sitting. Spirituality is not determined by how much of the Bible we read each day. The constant feedback we receive from grown young people goes something like this: "Our family worship was so boring! You know, Mom read on and on and on. Then Dad prayed on and on and on. We couldn't wait for it to end!"

My wife and I visited a family in Holland. The children spoke no English, yet they communicated well with us. After dinner we shared in their family worship time. There were three children: a preschooler, a first-grader, and a third-grader. Along with their mother, they pantomimed Scripture for us. We were told to watch carefully because we would have to interpret what they were acting out and no words would be spoken.

Spirituality is not determined by how much of the Bible we read each day.

First we witnessed a portrayal of the Parable of the Lost Sheep. Next they did Esther before Ahasuerus—that was a rough one! Finally they acted out the episode of Paul's imprisonment, with his nephew informing the authorities. You can imagine how long all of this took. We had to watch carefully. The impact that came through to us was how well they knew the stories and were able to project the ideas to us without words. Best of all, every one of us enjoyed the experience!

Family worship doesn't have to be boring to be biblical.

It's a crime to bore a person with the Word of God. Bore a person with Emerson or Shakespeare or nuclear physics, but not with the Bible! Use modern translations and paraphrases to transfer God's Word into words your children can digest and absorb—their heart language.

Guidelines for Meaningful Family Worship

What constitutes a meaningful worship time in the home? Admittedly, every home is different and family worship will vary, but there are basic guidelines you can follow to ensure that your family worship is an investment in eternity, not wasted time.

• *Make family worship age appropriate.* Generally children under the age of three or four who cannot sit still for a fifteen-minute family time should be excused. When many ages are involved, the content must be geared to the youngest age, but with keen appreciation of the needs of the oldest child.

• *Timing is not important, but regularity is.* Morning? Evening? It depends on your family. The time of day is less important than the fact that family worship is high priority in your home and will happen *every day* at whatever time you have chosen. Priority and regularity will rivet the critical importance of family worship into the minds and hearts of your children.

• *Be brief but not rushed.* Always include some portion of relevant Scripture, sometimes read from the Bible and other times recited from memory. Always have a time of prayer. Unless your children demonstrate strong interest in a particular topic of discussion or prayer, try to keep family worship times brief.

• *Strive for variety.* Obviously, different formats require creative planning. Consider options such as these:

The day after church services: Each person shares something learned during the worship service the day before.

Other weekdays: Devote time to missionaries. Read their stories; keep in contact with them by e-mail, tapes, or letters. There is a tiny part of Africa closer to our family than many parts of Dallas because our family made the needs of a Bible institute there our family concern.

Make your prayers specific: for relatives who are sometimes the hardest to reach with spiritual truth, for church and school friends, and for issues in the local community. Pray for public servants, for our nation's leaders, and for whatever concerns your family has.

Review Bible memory work, learn hymns of our faith, and sing together. Older children can plan worship times; in our home, we assigned days for each child. It provided excellent opportunities for them to play their musical instruments.

Don't be afraid to be original. Many books with creative ideas are available for families, but adapt resources to your own needs. Drama, videos, puppets, craft projects, and art can be introduced, for example.

• *Keep it casual.* We parents do not have to be preachy. In fact, we should avoid trying to lecture. We can make family worship a natural and primarily child-centered time of heart overflow. Family worship is a time to open the door of each heart and allow the Holy Spirit to speak.

Richard Baxter pastored a wealthy and sophisticated parish in Scotland. For three years he preached with passion but saw no visible results. Finally one day he threw himself across the floor of his study and cried out, "O God, You must do something with these people or I'll die!" It was as if God spoke audibly and said, "Baxter, you are working in the wrong place. You are expecting revival to come through your pulpit preaching. Try the home."

Baxter then went out and visited the home of every parishioner, spending entire evenings helping parents set up family worship times with their children. Then the Holy Spirit began little revival fires in one home after another. Finally those fires swept through the whole congregation and made his church the memorable body of believers it became. In the process, God made Baxter a man of godly distinction.

Ask God to bring revival into your home.

We hear much about the need for spiritual revival today, but it is almost always connected to a pulpit ministry. I wonder if God is saying to us, "You are working in the wrong place." Ask God to bring revival into your home. If He does, I guarantee that it will overflow into your church. Revival begins when you intentionally establish a value system—a priority—to meet the Lord every day with your family.

Remember, He is seeking our worship. Likewise, He is seeking to help you instill godly values in the hearts of your children. Through family worship, heaven can indeed help today's home.

RECOMMENDED READING FOR FAMILY WORSHIP

Preschool Children

Barrett, Ethel and Blankenbaker, Frances. *Our Family's First Bible Storybook* (Regal).

Beers, V. Gilbert. *My Picture Reading Book* (Victor).

Henley, Karyn. *The Beginner's Bible* (Zondervan).

Lindvall, Ella K. *The Bible Illustrated for Little Children* (Moody).

Lucado, Max. *Because I Love You* (Crossway).

Sattgast, L.J. *My Very First Bible* (Harvest House).

School Children

Erickson, Mary. *Learning About God from A to Z* (NavPress).

Jahsmann, Alan H. and Martin, Simon P. *Little Visits with God* (Concordia).

Lewis, C.S. *The Chronicles of Narnia* (HarperCollins).

Oyer, Sharron; Cannon, Kelly; and Torjussen, Jean. *Seekers in Sneakers* (Harvest House).

Taylor, Kenneth. *Devotions for the Children's Hour* (Moody).

Adolescents

Campbell, Stan. *BibleLog: Thru the Bible series* (Victor).

Davis, Ken. *How to Live with Your Parents without Losing Your Mind* (Youth Specialties).

Lewis, C.S. *The Chronicles of Narnia* (HarperCollins).

Realistic Devotions for Teens (Harold Shaw).

Pollock, John. *A Foreign Devil in China* (Worldwide Publications).

ten Boom, Corrie and John Scherrill. *The Hiding Place* (Bantam).

Missions

Elliot, Elisabeth. *Through Gates of Splendor* (Tyndale House).

Jolinstone, Patrick J. *Operation World* (WEC International).

Tucker, Ruth A. *From Jerusalem to Irian Jaya* (Zondervan).

When People Pray (Overseas Missionary Fellowship).

CHAPTER NINE

How to Upstage Today's Entertainment World

*"I came that they might have life,
and might have it abundantly."*
John 10:10

Every normal child living in twenty-first-century America encounters the make-believe world of colorful, sassy, and altogether appealing animals and imaginary creatures in books and on the screens of movies, television, and computers. Creative imagination is God's gift to little tots to help them cope with complexities in their lives. Dr. Selma Fraiberg, who wrote the classic text on early childhood (*The Magic Years,* Scribner, 1959), states that a child's imagination is important for his or her mental health. While imagination provides pleasure, it also helps them deal with fears and problems. Parents do well to allow little ones to employ their fanciful tools of imagination to grow a healthy preparedness for life.

Christian parents, however, should remember that the commercialized, fun world created for children is laced with subtle hooks designed to trigger an unhealthy consumerism. In addition, children's media often plant a furtive, philosophical seed of godless idolatry. For example, the immensely popular film and theater productions of Disney's *The Lion King* have delighted audiences of eager children with magnificent characters, costumes, and music. But the story line, which seems so benign as the young lion prince follows the sage advice given before his disobedience, is sprinkled with a New Age message of earth worship and total disregard for the fact that the magnificent world around him was made by the Creator God.

Although Christian families should not disassociate themselves from secular society, it is important to understand the intrusion of the entertainment world upon our lifestyles and philosophies—and the dominance it demands. In a perceptive look at popular culture titled *Dancing in the Dark* (Eerdmans, 1991), Quentin Schulze and his fellow professors of communications quoted from a speech made at the dedication of the $14 million cinema and television school at the University of California: "But for better or worse, the influence of the church, which used to be all-powerful, has been usurped by film. Films and television tell us the way we conduct our lives, what is right and wrong."

> *"If you don't come apart, you'll come apart."*

There is no question that we want to carefully monitor our children's formative thinking. We find ourselves resembling a clean-up crew, forever scrubbing away the soot of peer pressure, multimedia influence, and even some of the values taught in our school classrooms. Rearing a family certainly requires lots of stamina—physical, emotional, spiritual, and mental.

So we need time to relax, opportunities to recoup our strength and energy. With perceptive practicality, our Lord said to His tired men, "Come ye yourselves apart into a desert place, and rest a while" (Mark 6:31, KJV). Vance Havner once summed up that verse this way: "If you don't come apart, you'll come apart."

The wonderful irony is that as we step away to relax and recharge our batteries from the pressures of work and family, we actually draw closer to our spouse and children by experiencing new sights and adventures together and laughing and playing together—free from the usual distractions, pressures, and influences of everyday life. Such recreational times away from routine help instill positive values and memories that last a lifetime.

Ecclesiastes 3:4 reminds us there is a time to laugh. A few verses later we find this editorial of Solomonic wisdom:

> What does one really get from hard work? I have thought about this in connection with all the various kinds of work God has given to mankind. Everything is appropriate in its own time. But though God has planted eternity in the hearts of men, even so, many cannot see the whole scope of God's work from beginning to end. So I conclude that, first, there is nothing better for a man than to be happy and to enjoy himself as long as he can; and second, that he should eat and drink and enjoy the fruits of his labors, for these are gifts from God.
>
> Ecclesiastes 3:9–13, TLB

WHY IS FAMILY RECREATION IMPORTANT?

Family recreation is not a heavy subject, but it is quite heavy upon my heart. It may determine the future of your life and family, as well as the quality of both.

Psalm 16:11 says, "Thou wilt make known to me the path of life." How unfortunate, then, that Christianity is often caricatured as a way of death! No doubt about it, the enemy has promoted the idea that to be a Christian is, frankly, a drag and that to be spiritual or to walk with God is to be miserable.

Someone once defined a Puritan as "a person who suffers from an overwhelming dread that somewhere, sometime, somehow, someone may be enjoying himself." This rather extreme judgment is descriptive of the muddled mentality of some believers. Eternal life, the New Testament assures us, is more than a *quantitative* thing, an unending existence. The person in hell will have that! The life God offers is a *qualitative* thing, a new kind of life. It does not begin at death; it begins at birth—the new birth.

Check it out for yourself. John 17 lists seven characteristics of eternal life, and six of the seven refer to the here and now—present possession. So let's say goodbye to the pie-in-the-sky rhetoric. The abundant life Jesus promises is as much for the here-and-now as it is for eternity.

This new quality of life begins the moment the Lord enters and transforms our hearts at our invitation. Why? Psalm 16:11 gives two reasons: (1) "In Thy presence is fullness of joy; and (2) "In Thy right hand there are pleasures forever." There is not just joy, but a superabundant, inexhaustible supply of it. These pleasures are as exciting in retrospect as they are in prospect, and they are there for all who trust in Christ as their Savior and Lord.

John Locke, the great thinker who helped shape eighteenth-century philosophy, offers this idea on recreation: "Recreation belongs not to people who are strangers to business ... . The skill should be, so to order their time of recreation, that it may relax and refresh the part that has been exercised and is tired, and yet do something which, besides the present delight and ease, may produce what will *afterwards be profitable*" (italics mine).

We should never allow the enemy to promote the fiction among Christians that *If it's enjoyable, it must be sinful.* John 10:10 is an extremely profound verse in a remarkable context. Mark the sharp contrast between the thief and the shepherd. The thief comes for three things: to steal, kill, and destroy. That's *wreck-reation.* But the Shepherd (Jesus Christ) offers a refreshing alternative: "I came that they might have life, and might have it abundantly." On the basis of the Greek text, this can be translated, "life, I mean *really live."*

Many of us are afflicted with a lethal disease—a spongy view of the spiritual life. *Praying?* We think. *That's spiritual. Reading the Bible? That's good! Sharing my faith? Better yet!* But if I'm playing with my kids on the floor—that's not viewed as being spiritual. If I'm with my family on vacation, that's not spiritual. The kink in this distorted idea is that it doesn't stack up with what Paul says. He encourages believers to do *all* things to the glory of God. (See 1 Corinthians 10:31; Colossians 3:17, 23.)

In John Bunyan's ageless allegory, *Pilgrim's Progress*, Mr. Feeble-mind is the counterpart of too many modern Christians. Having been rescued from the giant Slay-good, he is encouraged to continue his journey with the pilgrims, but complains, "I am a man of weak and feeble mind ... . I shall like no laughing, I shall like no gay attire, I shall like no unprofitable questions. I am ... offended with that which others have a liberty to do ... . Sometimes if I hear someone rejoicing in the Lord, it troubles me because I cannot do so too."

RECREATION BRINGS VITALITY

Too many people do not enjoy the Christian life; they endure it. It's a grim scene. They really know nothing about the grace of God, that emancipation from the drudgery of living. Whether they are into legalism or license, they are slaves. It is only a grace-pervaded life, produced by the Spirit of God, that's balanced.

The "joy of the Lord" is a biblical principle too little taught and too seldom practiced. Joy is like an untapped vein of rich fuel. The book of Nehemiah records the remarkable story of the rebuilding of the walls of Jerusalem and the subsequent revival under the prophet Ezra. During the dedication ceremonies and celebrations, these leaders read the holy law and told the people, "Go eat of the fat, drink of the sweet ... . Do not be grieved, for *the joy of the LORD is your strength* ... . And all the people went away to eat, to drink ... and to celebrate a great festival, *because they understood the words*" (Nehemiah 8:10,12; emphases added).

God wants His children to have intervals of pleasure and enjoyment.

God wants His children to have intervals of pleasure and enjoyment. Why do we insist on labeling fun as sin? If I dropped into your house or apartment, the place ought to be resounding with laughter. Often our homes are roaring, but not with laughter.

At Dallas Seminary we once had two graduates who came from the same home. If I had to pick two men from our alumni who are making an impact for the Savior, I would choose these products of a humble peach-farm home in California. I stayed in that home and came away saying, "O God, reproduce this all over America."

Once I asked one of those young men, "Hey, Ed, what do you remember most about your father?"

He pondered my question for a moment, then replied,

"Two things—and interestingly enough, they appear to be contradictory. I used to have a paper route, and I had to get up at 4 A.M. I'd go by my father's room and the door would be cracked, and I'd see him on his knees in prayer. That made a profound impression on me. The second thing I remember is my father rolling on the floor with us kids in laughter."

What an invincible combination—on his knees in prayer and on the floor in laughter! By the way, what will your children remember you for?

RECREATION MEANS RENEWAL

I remember the day the great missionary-statesman of the last generation, Robert Hall Glover, gave an address in New York City entitled, "Things I Would Pack in My Missionary Trunk If I Were Returning to the Field." The first thing he mentioned was a sense of humor.

I almost fell off the pew. *That's not very spiritual,* I thought.

And then he told the sad story of a steady stream of men and women returning from the mission field because they had never developed the ability to laugh, particularly at themselves. The paths of Christian experience are strewn with the wreckage of brilliant and gifted people, greatly used of God, who never were able to laugh.

Recreation means renewal—a process of brightening the often-dull routines and burdensome responsibilities inevitable to modern life. We live in a society that is overstimulated and underexercised—a bad combination. Pressures build, and we must let off some steam. Work does not kill, but unrelieved pressure does.

Since we never completely get out from under pressure, one of our great tasks in life is learning to manage it. In his self-published devotional book, *Ecclesiastes,* Robert D. Foster included this wonderful poem by an unknown author:

> Slow me down, Lord. Ease the pounding of my heart by the quieting of my mind.

> Steady my unhurried pace with a vision of the eternal reach of time.

> Give me, amid the confusion of the day, the calmness of the everlasting hills.

> Break the tensions of my nerves and muscles with the soothing music of the singing streams that live in my memory. Help me to know the magical, restoring power of sleep.

> Teach me the art of taking minute vacations—of slowing down to look at a flower, to chat with a friend, to pat a dog, to read a few lines from a good book.

> Slow me down, Lord, and inspire me to send my roots deep into the soul of life's enduring values, that I may grow toward the stars of my greater destiny.

Recreation Unites the Family

The early church started in a home. There's no magnet like a home for purposes of unity. This is the place where you build relationships. It's very interesting to walk into the room of a good friend who is experiencing extreme grief. You've built a relationship over the years by laughing, playing, praying, and crying together. Now you don't have to say a word. Your eyes meet and your presence is enough. Too many young people, when I ask them what they remember about their homes, tell me only negatives; not nearly enough remember happy, enjoyable scenes. You can change that through frequent times of let-loose recreation together as a family.

A young adult should be able to say, "Wow! I can still remember when we used to get together and play games. Pop would be lost in it. I used to think, *There's my father, this great big leader, acting silly.* It was wonderful! I knew he was for real." You see, that's what draws a family together. That's the stabilizing influence that keeps a kid from going off the deep end. Be silly together! Don't ever forget to build the fortification of family fellowship through recreation.

IDEAS FOR FAMILY RECREATION

Here are some suggestions that can steer you toward meaningful, rejuvenating, family-building recreation. They've worked wonders in our family and in many families we know. Use them to stimulate your own creativity:

• *Take a day off and spend it with the family.* How about family fishing? Izaak Walton, the seventeenth-century fishing enthusiast, wrote, "We may say of angling as Dr. Boteler said of strawberries: 'Doubtless God could have made a better berry, but doubtless God never did.' And so, if I might be the judge, God never did make a more calm, quiet innocent recreation than angling."

• *Carve out a daily playtime with small children.* A little means a lot. Study your schedule to determine the best time of the day. And when you're with them, give them your full attention. Don't be afraid to be silly—these times may become some of your child's best memories as he or she grows older.

• *Designate a family night.* Let the family *decide* and *do* something for fun. We used to have the Hendricks Talent Theater—a homegrown comedy special that was always a hit. Try it yourself or come up with dozens of ideas of your own.

• *Have a family vacation.* Even a weekend is meaningful when you are saying with your actions, "I choose to spend this time with you." That says volumes about your priorities. And the memories you create together will be priceless.

• *Try a couples retreat.* Get away with other couples or just the two of you. Evaluate your family away from the scene of action. Set goals. Readjust your priorities.

• *Explore interfamily recreation.* Invite another family to your home—just for fun.

> *Family fun requires a free spirit as well as free time.*

Family fun requires a free spirit as well as free time. A free spirit escapes once in a while from the demands of life's regular routine. Jesus Christ warned, "Beware! Don't always be wishing for what you don't have. For real life and real living are not related to how rich we are" (Luke 12:15, TLB). Then He told the story of a prosperous but very foolish farmer. Although the point of the parable lies elsewhere, it gives us an example of a man who kept running an expansion program until he far outstripped anybody else in the neighborhood. When he decided to take a vacation, it was too late.

And More Ideas

- *Picnic at the lake* (watch sailboats, take a walk to find interesting keepsake stones, feed the ducks, play Frisbee).
- *Visit the zoo.*
- *Fly kites.*
- *Drive out of town* to see farm animals, pick wild flowers or leaves, find nuts or pine cones, or walk along a country lane.
- *Eat in a quaint restaurant.*
- *Rent a video* and pop popcorn.
- *Go jogging or biking.*
- *Tour historical sites.*
- *Celebrate your spouse's birthday* with a treasure hunt of small gifts around the home. (Let the kids help hide the gifts.)
- *Canoe down a river.*
- *Play table games at home.*
- *Look at old photographs* and share memories.
- *Visit museums and art galleries.*
- *Window-shop at the mall.*
- *Make "miss-you" cards* for friends and relatives who live far away.
- *Bake a pie together.*
- *Walk the dog.*
- *Play tennis or badminton.*
- *Visit a small airport* and watch planes come and go.
- *Create a table centerpiece.*
- *Go skating.*
- *Sing together.*
- *Read about antiques* and then visit antique stores.
- *Walk through a cemetery* and read the headstones.
- *Make candles.*
- *Play touch football in the park* or shoot baskets.

- *Learn archery.*
- *Camp out* at a state park.
- *Draw or paint.*
- *Create a family theater* with original script and costumes.
- *Draw a family tree.*
- *Plant a family garden.*
- *Learn new crafts* (ceramics, woodworking, flower arranging, rock polishing).
- *Train a dog.*
- *Take a mystery trip.*
- *Take walking or driving tours* published in your local newspaper.

DON'T SETTLE FOR "SOMEDAY"

Family recreation should be pulled off the dusty shelf of "things we would like to do someday" and put into working order today. Let me leave you with four simple suggestions to encourage you to make family recreation a regular part of your home life:

1. *Plan it.* We never plan to fail, but we do fail to plan.

2. *Vary it.* Avoid recreational ruts by incorporating all kinds of mental, physical, cultural, and social outlets.

3. *Provide for it.* Set aside small bits of money in a fancy container for family recreation. Even the children should drop in their tiny contributions. This small investment will pay life-long dividends.

4. *Think creatively.* Set up a "fun think tank" and come up with your own original ideas for family fun. Work at encouraging full participation instead of

spectatorship. As a parent, be involved, not just entertained.

Break the routine. Step outside the box. Laugh. Be silly. When you sprinkle recreational spice into your family's living patterns, you'll help counteract the exhaustion of everyday life as well as the negative influences of your children's culture. You'll draw closer as a family and create warm, precious memories for a lifetime.

Most of all, you'll affirm, for yourself and for your family, the truth of Jesus' words: "I came that they might have life, and might have it abundantly."

CHAPTER TEN

Heaven Help the Budget

What do you have that you did not receive?
1 Corinthians 4:7

Rattling its eerie bones periodically, a financial skeleton lurks in the closets of many Christian homes. Conservatively, it is estimated that more than half of all domestic problems are in some way related to financial misunderstandings or bad financial decisions. The inability or unwillingness of couples to address and solve financial issues is a major factor in America's high divorce rate.

I still remember a cartoon I saw years ago in which a coed said to her soon-to-be-wed friend, "I sure hope you have a happy marriage."

"Oh, we won't have any problems," replied the bride-to-be, "as long as we don't mention money." She was adding to her marriage vows an invisible exception: "Till debt do us part."

Debt can be a rising tide, or even a tidal wave, that sweeps unsuspecting families into a sea of treacherous obligations. Without careful thought and planning, few families can escape the clutches of credit-card debt and cash-flow concerns.

Our contemporary world demands involvement with money. That's why we need to pay particular attention to three aspects of family finances: (1) the biblical truth about money; (2) intelligent management of money; and (3) training our children how to deal with money.

We come into adulthood, and its responsibilities, largely influenced by our early home experiences and often an ill-defined philosophy about money. My parents' home, for example, strongly reflected the Great Depression and was all about saving—and spending as little as possible. My parents had a strong, independent, hard-working, no-frills ethic. Jeanne's early home training, however, while mirroring the same Great Depression, was more relaxed. In her view, it was okay to borrow from Peter to pay Paul. Budgets were made to be flexible and sometimes ignored. That created a recipe for discord in our marriage. Not until we sought out professional assistance did we resolve our deeply ingrained convictions about dollars and financial sense.

God's Word on Money

Jesus Christ had more to say about money than about heaven and hell combined. He knew money is a major component of everyday living and has to be faced squarely. Consider, for example, how he instructed Peter to pay the temple tax (Matthew 17:24–27) and styled most of His parables to relate to money management.

The Bible contains many examples, exhortations, commands, and warnings about money. God's Word denounces greed and extols generosity with strict honesty—with no apology for its financial emphases. First Corinthians 15, for example, highlights the resurrection theme, then chapter 16 addresses the collection of money. Is this contrast discordant? Not at all, because it takes resurrection power to get many Christians to give money! Fiscal stewardship may be the greatest reflection of resurrection reality at work.

CHRISTIAN STEWARDSHIP IS TOTAL, NOT PARTIAL

Everything you possess has its source in God. It is not what you do with the 10 or 20 percent you give that matters most, but rather what you do with the 80 or 90 percent you retain. Many Christians feel that by giving a small percentage they have obviously bypassed all other responsibilities and can do as they please with the remainder. Nothing is further from the truth of Scripture.

I think one of the most devastating errors revolves around much of what is taught under the heading of tithing. Tithing is presented frequently as if it is something you do in order to get, rather than something you do because of what you have received. A testimony I heard during a meeting of Christian businessmen remains vividly with me. "My business was just about to go under," one man shared, "and I wouldn't have made it. But I decided to tithe. I gave God 10 percent, and from then on my business has been flourishing. Every dollar I give to God, He gives me back two."

That's fantastic! How do you and I get in on that? I don't know a businessperson in America, or virtually anyone else for that matter, who wouldn't be interested in a deal that guarantees a 100 percent return on every dollar invested! Unfortunately, while that may be good human finances, it's not good biblical teaching. We are to give to God regardless of whether we go broke. Yet we cannot possibly outgive God. James 1:17 declares that every gift originates with God. His major characteristic, James assures us, is His constancy. The only kind of gift He knows how to give is a perfect one.

Paul raises the question in 1 Corinthians 4:7: "What do you have that you did not receive?" The correct answer can only be "nothing."

Years ago our family had a delightful little dachshund,

Franz. Half a dog high and two dogs long, Franz helped us raise four kids. What we appreciated most about him was his response when we brought his plate of food. He would almost leap out of his shiny black fur with excitement. He wagged his tail so much we thought his back end would come off. He sat up so beautifully and "spoke" (politely, of course) and licked our hands. He was smart enough to know where his food came from. That's smarter than many humans are today.

Everything you possess has its source in God.

"Why should I give thanks?" someone may ask. "After all, I earned the money with which to buy this food." Really? Where did you get the strength, the ability, and the breath you take every minute? Everything is sourced in God, and the grateful person not only recognizes it but gives thanks. We thank God not only with our prayers and acknowledgments, but also with our giving to the work of His kingdom.

GIVING IS AN INVESTMENT IN ETERNITY

In 2 Corinthians 9:6, we read more of this sowing-reaping metaphor: "He who sows sparingly shall also reap sparingly; and he who sows bountifully shall also reap bountifully." The choice in both cases is ours.

The Scriptures do not teach that money is always and only "filthy lucre." They explain that money is *fellowship* (see Philippians 1:3–5, 4:15; 2 Corinthians 8:1–5). Money is a form of sharing and communicating. I believe giving money is one of the most significant expressions of faith because one must give without the element of sight.

Have you ever been caught unprepared in a church or meeting when they passed the collection plate? You may have fumbled in your pocket or purse and thought, *My shattered nerves! I'm trapped! Nothing less than a ten-dollar bill! What a revolting development!* So you took the bill and kissed it good-bye.

May I suggest another alternative? Next time the plate goes by, remember that nothing else you have will endure after a period of time. But through the transmutation of spiritual phenomena, the money you give in faith to God is translated into terms of eternal currency. Ask yourself, *How is my heavenly stock portfolio? How many eternal securities do I own?*

REGULATE MONEY ACCORDING TO NEW TESTAMENT PRINCIPLES

A pattern is provided in 1 Corinthians 16:2. Giving is to be *regular:* "on the first day of every week." Every time the Lord's Day arrives, as this verse reveals, you have a reminder of your responsibility in giving.

Giving is to be very *personal.* This same verse continues, "... let each one of you put aside and save."

Giving is also to be *systematic.* This verse conveys a picture of a little pile of money that is reserved exclusively for God. It means that He is at the top of your priority list, regardless of whether you ever get to the rest of the list. Have you learned this yet?

We've all seen Christian people grasping erratically at ways to relax in our tense, materialistic world. "I gotta do something to relax!" they growl. Recklessly, they cut back or forsake their regular giving in order to invest in elaborate hobbies requiring complicated and costly equipment. A year later, bored of their new hobbies, they lose money when no one wants to buy their used diving outfits or splattered darkroom equipment. God has a fantastic ability to take our money, when it is gained and used contrary to His patterns, and pour it into a bag of holes. Have you discovered the leaks yet?

Giving is to be *proportionate.* Paul added, in 1 Corinthians 16:2, "as God hath prospered him" (KJV). Every time the Lord's Day rolls around, think of the divine prosperity in your life. "As God has prospered you" becomes the basis of your giving. This should transform your giving beyond recognition.

Attitude Is More Important than Amount

Jesus taught that how we use our money reveals so much about our character. Remember how He sat down opposite the treasury "and began observing how the multitude were putting money into the treasury" (Mark 12:41)? Why was He so fascinated? Because *our stewardship of money is a spiritual barometer,* a far more accurate index of our relationship to Jesus Christ than any other element including prayer, Bible reading, and sharing our faith with others. All of these we can do and still have a self-centered spirit. But this is not so with giving—at least not as it is described here.

"Many rich people were putting in large sums. And a poor widow came and put in two small copper coins, which amount to a cent" (Mark 12:41–42).

Jesus called His disciples to Him and said, "Truly I say to you, this poor widow put in more than all the contributors to the treasury" (v. 43). It's as if Jesus is saying, "Drink it in! You won't see this very often!"

It's obvious that He was not impressed with the amount she gave; we've already been told she gave the smallest denomination of currency. He was talking about attitudes. The scribes put in their money out of their excess, but she threw in all that she had. If anybody had a legitimate reason for keeping something back, this woman did. Yet she gave it all away, and Jesus Christ said, in effect, "Gentlemen, that is worth observing."

I can still remember from boyhood that my grandmother, who knew Christ as her Savior, often repeated this little couplet that sort of dinned its way into my mind:

It's not what you'd do with a million,
If a million were your lot;

It's what you are doing at present
With the dollar and a quarter you've got.

Sometimes I hear students say, "When I get out of school, I'll give ... ." What a sorry excuse for not giving. The real question we each need to ask ourselves is, *What am I doing with what I now have?* God looks on the heart. First Timothy 6:10 says, "For the love of money is a root of all sorts of evil." The snag is not the money but the motive behind how we use it.

Give First

Budgets should flow from family prayer, family planning, and periodic evaluation. Christ said, "Where your treasure is, there will your heart be also" (Luke 12:34). We likely would have written it in reverse: "It's just common sense—where your affections reside, your money will be pressing in close behind." The young lover buys his girlfriend flowers or jewelry. The sportsman mortgages his income for several years in order to buy an imposing boat. But Christ knows the human heart. He asks for an act of the will *first.* That's where the act of giving comes in.

Does it sometimes bother you that many Christian enterprises around the world languish while Christians live in luxury? It is not our place to judge our brother or sister who may have a higher standard of living than our own. But it is appropriate to ask, "What are we willing to do without so that the Gospel might be spread and believers strengthened?"

Of one thing Christians can be sure: God has promised to supply *all* of our needs. He who fed five thousand and turned water into wine for thirsty wedding guests will provide for us. Sometimes, however, He may also let us suffer lack of resources because we have chosen to slight His commands to provide for those in need and for those in Christian ministry.

Giving develops the giver. That is one reason God ordained that His work be financed by the gifts of His people. Our Lord is not only our Supplier; He is also our Investment Counselor who provides infallible financial advice. Following Him won't guarantee a healthy dollar profit, but it will guarantee healthy spiritual dividends.

Curb Impulse Spending

Like a volatile gas, money must be carefully managed. It must be stored in a leak-proof container and measured out in proper quantities. It must be directed, applied, and accounted for. In other words, we need to keep financial records.

Inadequate records are a primary cause of overspending. Nearly everyone agrees that at least a rough budget must be made, but what happens to the "miscellaneous" section? The money spent impulsively? Many homes are shattered on the rocks of impulsive spending. The key to steering through this channel? Agreement between the husband and wife. Who should keep the records? The husband? The wife? The question is not so much *who* as *how* the finances will be managed. The one best suited for, and more inclined toward, arithmetic and detail work should assume this task. The family budget should be determined by need, not wants. The black-and-white, unemotional facts should be laid out: amount of income, places of distribution, the agreed-upon value system, and so on. In our family, for example, we have always placed education among our priorities. We will go without something else in order to buy significant reading material or pay school tuition. My wife finished her college degree after we had four children. The only way we could work it out was through her attendance at a private university that charged a substantial rate for tuition. We budgeted that tuition because we agreed that her degree was more important at that particular time than a new car, a bigger house, or the latest-style clothes.

> *Of one thing Christians can be sure: God has promised to supply all of our needs.*

Don't believe all the ads. Professional economists report that the most thorny matters relating to money for young people are rooted in advertising. That is a good word of warning. Avoid comparing and coveting. Don't feel sorry for yourself. Face up to the limits of your resources, including your anticipated income, and then decide what you can do without. Flee unnecessary luxuries. A money management expert once advised, "Don't try to climb the Himalayas when your income is better suited to the Adirondacks."

List your needs, survey your situation, and draw up a rough budget. Set your major goals by mutual consent.

Decide together how you will deal with credit-related issues. Also do a periodic financial review and adjust as needed.

Train Children to Deal with Money

My father used to ask, "Do you think money grows on trees?" Most children think it grows on Dad! Children soak up parental attitudes toward money like a blotter. So it is important for you to begin early as a parent to model what you'd like them to do years later.

The first few dimes and quarters make lasting impressions. Children should have allowances for which they are accountable. There will be casualties. Many years ago our first child, Barb, desperately wanted to buy a cheap necklace of plastic pearls, mostly because she admired what her neighbor friend had. Against her mother's advice, Barb spent most of her small allowance for the necklace. Not surprisingly, the very first day she wore it the pearls broke—landing all over the back of the station wagon as we drove home from church. That afternoon she crawled onto my lap, lavished me with kisses, and finally said softly, "Daddy, I guess I shouldn't have bought the pearls." She twisted her face into a disgusted expression and spat out the word, "Cheap!"

Events such as this one provide bargain education for minimal tuition—if we learn from them. Unfortunately, many young people drop out of higher education because they have misspent thousands of dollars, having never learned to weigh true value against compulsory spending.

Don't hesitate to teach your child the law of natural consequences. The few dollars the child wastes during the first days of the allowance period is an investment in practical education if he or she comes to understand the importance of thinking before spending. He or she may complain bitterly—and you may be tempted to bail out the foolish spender. Don't do it.

Our son had a paper route, getting up at 4 A.M. to deliver dailies for an entire month. At the end of the month, he was in a deep financial hole. I had always warned him, "Watch the draw!" That is, if someone does not pay or you have more papers than customers, cut down your order. But he was careless about these things and somewhat intimidated by a super-salesman boss, so he paid a painful price. Many years later I asked him what he had learned about money while growing up. "Watch the draw!" was his quick reply.

Encourage every child by providing a program of work and careful investment of every dollar he or she earns. I never get paid for mowing my lawn. Jeanne receives no money for cooking dinners. These are teamwork necessities. But I did pay my children for special chores such as washing the car or completing a time-consuming special project.

> *Don't hesitate to teach your child the law of natural consequences.*

As my children grew up, my wife and I always tried to keep a mental list of earning possibilities for them, teaching the principle that a laborer is worthy of his wages (Luke 10:7).

Encourage your children to work for someone outside the family. Did you ever wait tables in a restaurant? It'll provide a liberal arts education! (I jokingly remind my young friends that I don't think a person should have a license to get married until he or she has waited tables.) A job gives a young person the opportunity to give first, save systematically, and spend wisely.

It's More Blessed to Give

When all is said and done, God expects us to be wise stewards of the money He entrusts to us. And it all starts with obeying Him by giving. Give generously to those in need with a willing and trusting spirit if God asks you to do so. Then carefully manage the rest, always paying your bills on time and setting aside a portion for future needs and dreams.

A small boy was given two coins and instructed that one was for the church collection and the other was for an ice-cream cone. As he ran down the street enthusiastically, he dropped one, and it rolled into a sewer. "Well, Lord, there goes your dime!" he exclaimed. We chuckle, but that is precisely what many of us are doing—assigning to God what we lose or mismanage. The way we treat our temporal resources will always reflect how much we value our spiritual riches. The rule of our financial lives should always be the words of our Lord: "It is more blessed to give than to receive" (Acts 20:35).

Evangelist Luis Palau tells how he was particularly moved by a crucial need he learned about while traveling. He went home and told his wife that he had pledged one thousand dollars during the next year for this need. From a missionary's personal budget, this was a staggering sum! Together the Palaus prayed and agreed to trust the Lord for the amount. During the year, they received an inheritance from a family member for that very amount—completely unforeseen! God always honors the faith of the person who steps out in faith according to His will.

For further reading: *Raising Money-Smart Kids,* Ron and Judy Blue, Thomas Nelson, 1991.

CHAPTER ELEVEN

Survival Training for the Sex Jungle

*For you have been bought with a price:
therefore glorify God in your body.*
1 Corinthians 6:20

From Madison Avenue to junior high locker rooms, it seems as if everyone is freely talking about sex. Copywriters use it to sell everything from cars to mouthwash. Sexual overtones and double entendres lace everyday speech. Even our healthcare industry has splattered sex across major media outlets. It's no secret that dark perversions are seeping into our classrooms and pervade many computer websites. Consequently, countless young people are getting lost in what I call "the sex jungle."

Faced with these challenges, many Christian parents are too stunned, too threatened, or too timid to assume the role of sex educators, a responsibility that should rest on their shoulders. Many moms and dads still stammer and stir their coffee with a fork when their children ask certain questions. Otherwise-talkative grandparents suddenly have an urge to walk the dog or call the cat when confronted with a little child's query about how fathers figure into the birth process. But there's no getting around the fact that we parents are the only ones truly qualified to protect the welfare of our children's sexual well-being.

When Jeanne was little, she was riding in a car full of

relatives on a beautiful spring morning. As they drove past a field where a flock of sheep were feeding, she saw a ram mounted on the back of a ewe. With childish curiosity she asked her dad, sitting next to her, what the sheep were doing. Jeanne has never forgotten her dad's uncharacteristic response. He didn't say a word, just gave her a sharp elbow to the ribs. That gesture clearly conveyed a message. She still wasn't exactly sure what the sheep were doing, but she knew that either they shouldn't have been doing it or she shouldn't have asked about it.

Sexual questions are as normal to children as scientific questions. "Why is there a ring around the moon tonight?" the child wonders aloud. Question time is teaching time. It is an invitation to step into the child's private thought world—simply, directly, and naturally—and build the foundation for a healthy, respectful attitude toward sexuality as the wondrous creation God intended it to be.

Unfortunately, parents often conduct sex education as if they were preoccupied motorists. They sail right past the stop signs and sit like stalled cars in front of green lights.

Why should we be ashamed to discuss what God was not ashamed to create? Consider what Dr. Lester Kirkendall, distinguished former professor of family life at Oregon State University, wrote in his book *Learning to Love:*

> Most people assume that in the absence of direct instruction no sex education takes place. Actually the parents' reaction to themselves and to each other as sexual beings, their feelings toward the child's exploration of his own body, their attitude toward the establishment of toilet habits, their response to his questions and his attempts to learn about himself

and his environment, their ability to give and express their love for each other, and for him, are among the many ways they profoundly influence the child's sexual conditioning ... . The fact cannot be escaped. Parents cannot choose whether or not they will give sex education; they can choose only whether they will do something positive or negative about it, whether they will accept or deny their responsibility.

It may be easy for some of us to imagine a high-pitched voice from the fourth row calling out, "But, Professor, it just isn't done in our family. We don't talk about intimate things. I think it's in poor taste." So let's look at ways you can communicate positive attitudes and information about sex to your child.

The Importance of Parental Modeling

Start first not with what you say, but with what you do. Family structure enhances learning about life. Ponder the Old Testament example of the Israelites:

And you shall teach them [words from God] diligently to your sons and shall talk of them when you sit in your house and when you walk by the way and when you lie down and when you rise up ... . When your son asks you in time to come, saying, "What do the testimonies and the statutes and the judgments mean which the LORD commanded you?" then you shall say to your son, "We were slaves to Pharaoh in Egypt, and the LORD brought us from Egypt with a mighty hand" (Deuteronomy. 6:7, 20-21).

Just as the commandments of God were (and are) best taught in the home, so is sex education primarily and ideally the parents' responsibility—and best communicated in the context of home relationships.

Think of each member of your family as a point on the edge of a circle. Draw an imaginary line from each family member to every other one. Each line is a two-way street for learning as the family lives together—learning that forms an attitude toward sex as well as other aspects of living. Between parents, between parents and children, and between brothers and sisters, important interaction is taking place. The family is a built-in, automatic teaching device!

As parents, we are to provide the model from which our children will learn basic attitudes and knowledge about sex. This is why I believe that, in two-parent families, the best sex education you can ever give your child is to love your spouse; single parents teach healthy sex education by speaking with nothing but high respect toward the absent parent and toward the opposite sex in general.

What You Need to Know About Sex

What does a parent need to know in order to receive his or her teaching certificate in sex education? Let me suggest eight crucial guidelines.

1. Provide Consistent, Warm Affection

A child must experience from birth a warm (but not a smothering) affection from both parents that involves touch. Balanced giving and receiving of love is a basic stabilizer of life. A loving parent keeps giving even when tired, busy, sick, bored, or whatever else may tug him or her away from this primary responsibility. The affection must be given out appropriately according to the personality and needs of the child.

Jeanne recalls the day when, as a small child, she was being driven home from an all-day picnic. Dirty and sunburned, she awakened reluctantly as the car pulled into the garage. Before her father even unpacked the car, he carried her upstairs and put her into a tub of warm water. He understood that this was no time to play funny bath-time games. In practically no time, he had gently dried her, smoothed lotion on her sunburn, and tucked her between the sheets.

The love and warm, tender affection of Jeanne's father made a permanent impression on her. Guess what Jeanne did with our own little tykes, decades later, after an all-day outing?

2. Show Your Children that Their Parents Are in Love

Children should have no doubt that their parents are deeply in love with each other and unashamed to demonstrate that love [appropriately] in the presence of their children. Love is to be a way of life, woven into the fabric of family living—not a glossy finish that cracks when bent but a dyed-in-the-wool hue that pervades your whole home. How do children catch this? Like chicken pox—from exposure!

Some years ago Jeanne and I were embracing in our living room when our younger son, Bill, began plowing through the front door with his buddy from down the street.

"Shucks! We'll have to wait a minute," Bill quipped.

"Why?" his friend asked.

"Aw, my parents are in there smooching again. This goes on all the time!"

"Well, let's go in! Boy, it must be great to have a dad who loves your mom. I don't even know which one my father is. Every night we have a different dude in our house."

Caution! Don't evaluate your expressions of love to your spouse on the basis of children's reactions—especially if they are teens. "Yuck!" or "Here we go again!" may be their response, but the impact is on the inside—and it's positive.

"Aw, my parents are in there smooching again," Bill said. *"This goes on all the time!"*

In counseling, the most tragic words we hear are, "I can never remember once seeing my father embracing my mother." Along these lines, what are you giving your child as a heritage to remember?

Young children learn through their ever-curious senses: hearing, seeing, smelling, touching, and tasting. Their senses are ready-made to detect either love or complacency. Mom can hand a cup of coffee to Dad with a mute attitude that is frostbitten around the edges, or she can plant a small kiss on his head and say softly, "Here, Honey, I brought home this hazelnut coffee just for you." Her actions and words can release an emotional air freshener.

3. Teach and Model Healthy Sexual Identity and Respect

Help each child to identify with his or her own sex while respecting the opposite sex. Sex is far more than an act, a process of reproduction, or a biological phenomenon. It involves our total sexuality as persons. It's what makes a man a man and a woman a woman.

Children pick up attitudes like a vacuum cleaner inhales dirt. For example, a woman who cuts down men in her conversations is revealing more than she cares to admit about her own marriage. Sarcasm has no place in a good marriage. The husband who sneeringly remarks as his wife is looking in the mirror, "That's an exercise in futility," is in effect pouring sulfuric acid on his marriage. Magnify your mate before your family. "Man, it's great to have a daddy (or mommy) like ours!" communicates so much to a child.

It is a beautiful and wholesome scene when a woman looks at her little girl and says, "You know, it's great to be your mommy." Teach your children that what they are (male or female) is by the will of God. Encourage them by your example to develop an innate pride in their gender.

A distressing cultural phenomenon for today's Christian family is the degree to which homosexuality is portrayed as a positive and even "normal" form of sexual expression. We must never forget that homosexuality is an offense to God. Homosexuality mars His image (Genesis 1:27) and denies His plan for marriage (Genesis 2:24). In fact, God specifically forbids it, labeling it an abomination to God (Leviticus 18:22; 20:13).

Understand, however, that the New Testament clearly reveals that God offers mercy and forgiveness to any persons who break that commandment (1 Corinthians 6:9–11). As followers of Christ, we are to love people who sin sexually and help them find resolution for their disturbed emotions. We should also be intelligently informed about physiological and emotional addictions to sex. Ultimately, however, we must steer our children toward making healthy, biblically-sound decisions that will one day lead to sexual fulfillment within marriage or joyful lives of singleness if that should be God's plan.

The solution to the sex jungle is implicit in the

Scriptures. The lordship of Christ must reign over the realm of sex as over every other part of life. Paul cautions us, "Do you not know that your body is ... not your own? For you have been bought with a price: therefore glorify God in your body" (1 Corinthians 6:19–20).

4. Tell It Like It Is

If you are teaching a child to make cookies, you do not say, "Now we'll get those thingamajigs out of the drawer to measure the baking powder, then we'll use the whatchamacallit to sift flour." You teach correct names because the child needs to learn them. With a young child, you do not go into the technical jargon about the chemical changes in the baking of the cookie. You proceed on a simple, appropriate level.

So it is with the facts of intimate life. We should name the parts of the body when it is appropriate to do so. For example, breastfeeding of an infant should be referred to normally and naturally. As the child grows older, he or she should learn that a newborn actually begins life in a place called the uterus, and that when the baby is ready to be born it descends through the vaginal opening. This simple explanation lends confidence to the young child who is consumed with curiosity. Think how we've confused our children by telling them, in effect, "You're too young to ask that!" and then, a few years later, said, "You're old enough to know better!"

Bits and pieces of sex-related information picked up on the playground can easily be warped and distorted. When your child uses a word or expression that is questionable, we recommend you respond in a calm, matter-of-fact manner, "Where did you hear that? Do you know what it means? Let's look it up in the dictionary."

Then, together, look it up! This will enable you to tell it like it is, explain things parent-to-child, and field any questions your child may have. Then, make a standing offer: "Whenever you want to know the answer to a question, come to me; I'll give you the real picture."

Attitude and relationship, though, are far more important than *information* in sex education. The uptight, fear-ridden parent is poorly equipped to help his or her child. Embarrassment over sexual issues will only provide a negative role model. The universal lament of teens is, "I can't talk with my parents!"

> *Parents need to think ahead about how to handle simple questions.*

The highly sensitive, personalized subject of sex needs to be verbalized first between the parents themselves. Then discussion with the child won't be so uncomfortable. Parents need to think ahead about how to handle simple questions.

Let's say a three-year-old comes running in shouting, "Hey! Where do babies come from?" If Mom or Dad responds with an embarrassed "Not now, Honey!" they implant an unfortunate first impression that sexuality is not to be contemplated or talked about. Instead of a hushed reprimand, they should respond with appreciation: "I'm glad you asked." Then, after an age-appropriate explanation of God's design (see point 5 below), they should check up: "Is that what you wanted to know? Does that help?"

5. Tell the Truth, But Not Necessarily the Whole Truth

A little boy asked his mother where he came from, and also where she came from as a baby. His mother gave him a tall tale about a beautiful, white-feathered bird. The boy ran into the next room, asked his grandmother the same question, and received a variation of the bird story. He then scampered outside to his playmate and stated, "You know, there hasn't been a normal birth in our family for three generations!"

Usually a child does not want all of the truth at once. He or she is not interested in knowing all about lovemaking or reproduction. The child only wants a simple, direct answer to his or her question, and that is all that you should give. Always tell the truth, but not necessarily the whole truth. Don't tell more than your child wants or needs to know.

Such discussions are great opportunities to convey the wholesome wonder and mystery of God's plan. When God made Eve, He put Adam to sleep, and it is still a mystery to all of us how He actually did it. Likewise, sexual relationships remain an enigma, despite the glaring focus of the sexologists' spotlight. Quiet awe with reverence and sensitivity should infiltrate your teaching about sex, lest your child develop a coarseness and start using words in the wrong context just to demonstrate that he or she knows about life. Children need to grasp a holy awe, a deep respect, good taste, and a profound sense of thankfulness to God when learning about sex.

Yes, learning about sex involves an understanding of physiological facts of reproduction and warnings about unwanted pregnancies and sexually transmitted diseases. But in the Christian home, all of this information must be undergirded with a strong awareness that the body is the temple of the Holy Spirit. We are created by God and for His glory. We are "fearfully and wonderfully made" (Psalm 139:14). God's Word makes clear that sex between a married couple is an intimate, indescribable mystery full of wonder and joyful ecstasy. It also makes clear that anything else is a misuse of sex and offensive to our holy God.

6. Avoid Conveying Shame or Guilt

As children explore their sexuality, carefully avoid communicating shame and guilt.

Toilet training, for example, is often a time when parents inadvertently shame children or make them feel guilty about aspects of sexuality. Little Jimmy is proud of himself. After dinner he runs into the bathroom to urinate. Forgetting to hitch up his small trousers, he dashes back to Mommy in front of all the guests, announcing, "I did it all by myself!" With neither scolding nor embarrassment, Mom should sweep him up, take him back to the bathroom, and tell him as she replaces his pants, "We always put our clothes back on when we come out of the bathroom. I'm very proud of you."

Almost every home with a son and a daughter ends up with an exploratory experience sometime. It's not hard to imagine little Stevie, for example, wandering into the bathroom while his sister is bathing. He bounds out and announces, "Mommy, she's broken." Don't panic, just calmly use this as an opportunity to simply explain the God-designed differences between boys and girls. (In the process, you can underscore the courtesy of not walking into a bedroom or bathroom when the door is closed.)

As a parent, it's important for you to anticipate the needs of your growing child. A daughter approaching puberty should learn that "a most wonderful thing is going to happen" as she approaches her first menstrual cycle, but instruction shouldn't stop there. Calmly, parents should share precisely what is going to happen so that the daughter will not be alarmed when the first cycle begins. She needs to know not only what to expect, but that the menstrual cycle is a normal, God-designed part of growing to womanhood.

A young boy approaching puberty also needs knowledge and understanding. Parents should sit down and talk with him, calmly explaining what is happening in his body, how God is preparing him for something meaningful in his future, and that he doesn't want to ruin it by stepping outside of God's plan.

One lady asked me, "What do I do if I walk in and my son is masturbating?"

Some nights the boy will have nocturnal emissions and he will try to hide the fact. But wise moms and dads won't even mention it; they'll wash his underwear, pajamas or sheets while he's gone and let him know by their attitudes and actions that they love and believe in him and that what he's going through is a normal part of growing up.

One lady asked me, "What do I do if I walk in and my son is masturbating?" Answer: Just close the door. (She should have knocked first anyway.) Christians often teach that self-stimulation to achieve an erotic experience is sinful. Undoubtedly, especially with most young boys, it is an experimental pastime. My judgment is that a father should address the subject with his young sons, explaining how to deal with the pressures that lead to this activity so that it does not become a destructive habit. Accurate information is key in helping children understand and deal with the unfamiliar reproductive aspects of their bodies as they grow into adulthood. Just knowing the fact that "I do not belong to myself, but to God" (see 1 Corinthians 6:19,20) undergirds a positive attitude.

7. Use the "Teachable Moments" in God's Creation

We used to have a honey-colored female cocker spaniel that had sex with a young canine in the neighborhood and gave birth to puppies in our backyard. It was an event of first-rate educational value for our children. At first we watched from the family room window, then we moved to a respectful distance in the yard. Mama dog tugged at each newborn puppy, licked it from head to toe, and then gave it the final smell test to validate family odor. Witnessing all of this was a worship experience for our four year old, who looked up at me and exclaimed, "Wow!"

As appropriate, capitalize on the many opportunities in God's creation to teach your children about sex: the breeding of pets, the arrival of new babies, and so on. Visit a health museum. Buy well-illustrated books. Always help children relate what they're seeing or reading to God's creative love: "Isn't it great how God designed dogs to make puppies?" or "God loves us so much that He gives mommies and daddies the gift of having children together" can go a long way toward linking God's design to the facts of reproduction.

8. Warn Against Sexual Deviations

Children need to learn very early about our world's ever-increasing sexual dangers. We do not have to scare them, but we do need to make them aware. They will ask questions as they see billboards, newspapers, and television items that provoke their thinking.

Inform them that sexual deviates are often predatory and often seek converts. Rides with strangers are a no-no under any circumstances. Young children should be especially prepared to refuse "creative" approaches such as "I'm looking for my lost dog. Come over to my car and I'll show you his picture" or "Your mom's busy and told me to come by and pick you up from school."

A normal child, from an accepting and loving home, will have a natural aversion for deviates. One day when Jeanne was a child, she was walking home from school alone. As little girls will do, she tried to measure her steps with those of a man who was also walking through the park. When they reached a secluded section, he beckoned to her and began to unfasten his trousers. But she was not in the least interested in what he had to show her. Instead, she instinctively ran for home as fast as she could—a normal reaction for a normal child.

Healthy, God-centered sex education in the home is not optional; it's a critical necessity.

Today merchants of menace are pouring out lewd materials at an alarming rate, and much of it is accessible to our children. It is virtually impossible to shield children from all sexual propaganda, including that passed off as being factual information. The best protection you can provide your children is to clearly warn against pornography before they come across it—because they will! Back up your proactive training with a consistent upbringing of positive, loving care that helps build a healthy self-concept and teaches them to think, evaluate, and make wise judgments. We cannot change the fact that our world has diluted and degraded sex and bent it all out of God's intended shape, but as we help our children feel secure in their God-given sexuality they will have a natural aversion to deviant influences.

What else can parents do?

• Unless you live in a cave, your child most likely has

Internet access. Go online and utilize your service provider's parental controls to keep your child from accessing pornographic Web sites. Better yet, use a filtered Internet service provider. And *always* monitor your child when he or she is online.

• Your television is another source of increasing sexual content and foul language. From a child's early years on up, parents should proactively set and enforce clear rules regarding the amount and nature of TV to be watched. Be especially aware of cable networks that broadcast inappropriate sexual imagery day and night, and primetime network shows that take pride in "pressing the envelope" with obscenity, overt innuendo, brief nudity, and sexual acts.

• As your children get older, initiate discussions about drugs, abortion, homosexuality, AIDS, venereal disease, unmarried partners living together, and other topics they will undoubtedly confront.

IT'S NEVER TOO LATE

A teenage girl approached me after I spoke to her group and asked, "What's so wrong about having sexual relations with the boy I love, as long as it's 'safe sex'?" Her question revealed one of the abysmal flaws in contemporary sex education. There is no such thing as "safe sex." Not only are contraceptives unreliable, but she would also give away far more than her virginity. She would carry emotional baggage, assume responsibility she is not prepared for, and face consequences for the rest of her life.

Survey after survey has shown that the one area in which Christian young people feel least prepared for adulthood is the area of sex. Healthy, God-centered sex education in the home is not optional; it's a critical necessity.

Don't be embarrassed or afraid. Review the advice of this chapter, back it up with some additional reading, ask God to guide you, then be proactive. You'll do your children a big favor as you prepare them for the questions and issues they're going to face.

SEX EDUCATION RESOURCES

Jones, Stan and Brenda, *How and When to Tell Your Kids About Sex* (NavPress)

> Ages 3–5: *The Story of Me*
> Ages 5–8: *Before I Was Born,* by Carol Nystrom
> Ages 8–10: *What's the Big Deal?*
> Ages 11–14: *Facing the Facts*

Ketterman, Grace H., *How to Teach Your Child about Sex* (Revell).

Learning About Sex: A Series for the Christian Family (Concordia).

> Ages 3–5: *How to Talk Confidently with Your Child About Sex and Why Boys and Girls Are Different*
> Ages 6–8: *Where Do Babies Come From?*
> Ages 8–11: *How You Are Changing*
> Ages 11–14: *Sex and the New You*
> Ages 14+: *Love, Sex, and God*

McDowell, Josh and Day, Dick. *Why Wait?* (Thomas Nelson).

Niekler, John. *God, Sex, and Your Child* (Thomas Nelson).

Short, Ray. *Sex, Dating, and Love* (Augsburg).

Stafford, Tim. *A Love Story: Questions and Answers on Sex* (Tyndale House).

Wood, Barry. *Questions Teenagers Ask About Dating and Sex* (Revell).

CHAPTER TWELVE

Unless the Lord Builds the House ...

*For God has not given us a spirit of timidity,
but of power and love and discipline.*
2 Timothy 1:7

When you first began to turn the pages of this book, you were reminded that the Lord God Himself is the only contractor who knows how to construct a Christian home. "Unless the LORD builds the house," the psalmist writes, "they labor in vain who build it" (Psalm 127:1).

There are two contributors to the home-construction job: the builder (the Lord) and the laborers (Mom and Dad). Both are important. In fact, both are indispensable. God is the original architect and designer of the home and family; He knows the plans. For the actual fabrication, He uses a select group of workers. The quality of the finished product depends not so much on the skill of the laborers, but on their devotion and obedience to the builder. If we do not follow the Lord's direction, all of the skill we may bring to the job will be in vain.

KNOW WHERE YOU'RE GOING

Let's say you walk up to the airline ticket counter and ask for a ticket. "Where to?" the agent inquires.

"Oh, anywhere."

Ludicrous, right? Yet many of us are guilty of building a

marriage and a home without any specific objectives in mind. Many families are like sand dunes—they are shaped not by purpose, but by outside influences. Paul writes, "Let each man be careful *how* he builds" (1 Corinthians 3:10, italics added).

I was invited to speak in a church and, as I took my place behind the pulpit, I noticed a little sign on the pulpit facing me: WHAT IN THE WORLD ARE YOU TRYING TO DO TO THESE PEOPLE?

I later asked the pastor about it. "Well," he said, "I had been preaching here for seventeen years when I realized I had no goal, no objectives, in my preaching. I put up that sign to remind myself to have aims and to stick to them."

When we lose sight of our goals, we concentrate on our motions, like the pilot who announced to his passengers, "I'm afraid we are lost, but cheer up; we are making good time."

In ten years, what will you wish you had done today?

We cannot solve our problems unless we can see them. Proverbs 27:23 encourages vigilance: "Know well the condition of your flocks." And the New Testament frequently reminds us to know what's going on, as in these examples: "Let each one examine his own work" (Galatians 6:4); "Examine yourselves" (2 Corinthians 13:5). The Bible teaches spiritual quality control for the purpose of producing a superior product.

I once visited an office in which this sign was posted: **In ten years what will you wish you had done today?** DO IT NOW! That's good advice for Christian homebuilders. We need to form a mental image now of what we want our homes and children to be like ten years from now.

Clear objectives determine outcomes. You will accomplish that for which you aim. Aristotle said: "Like archers, we shall stand a far greater chance of hitting the target if we can see it."

I have never met a couple who *planned* a mediocre marriage and family. Just keep drifting, however, and you may have the dubious distinction of doing just that. Mediocre marriages or fractured families are the result of good intentions but poor implementation.

Many businessmen have shared with me their plans for the future of their businesses. Every day their efforts go into looking forward and strategizing a decade or more into the future. This same principle applies to families. As parents, we are not so much looking to produce good children as we are earnestly seeking to produce good adults. The results depend on what we do *today*.

This truth is perhaps best expressed by Jim Collins, author of the best-selling book, *Good to Great* (HarperCollins, 2001) and former professor at Stanford University Graduate School of Business:

> When all these pieces come together, not only does your work move toward greatness, but so does your life. For, in the end, it is impossible to have a great life unless it is a meaningful life. And it is very difficult to have a meaningful life without meaningful work. Perhaps then you might gain that rare tranquility that comes from knowing that you've had a hand in creating something of intrinsic excellence that makes a contribution.

The parenting business is all about producing adults who live to glorify God by contributing in meaningful ways to the world in which He has placed them. Therefore, our daily parenting must move toward clearly defined goals, not hazy dreams. Children dream (and they should), but their aspirations need guidance.

Who can forget the classic imagery captured by Richard Bach in his book *Jonathan Livingston Seagull?* As a loner seagull developing absurd flying skills, Jonathan hears his mother asking, "Why, Jon, why? Why is it so hard to be like the rest of the flock? Why don't you eat, son, you're bones and feathers."

"I don't mind being bone and feathers, Mom, I just want to know what I can do in the air and what I can't, that's all. I just want to know."

This exchange captures the exhilaration of youth, their need to spread their wings and explore their world. Every healthy child wants to grab the controls of life and make it work better than anyone else ever did. Parents are God's guidance system for them. What an opportunity—and what a challenge!

Niagara Falls is simply a phenomenon of nature—tons of water pouring over a dramatic drop in the earth's surface—*unless* that energy is harnessed, unless a hydroelectric plant seizes upon the power and puts it to work. Likewise, our families generate limitless resources that may go unused and unchanneled unless we parents skillfully harness them for definite purposes. What an opportunity—and what a challenge!

If we follow God's design and seek His daily guidance, we can do it!

MAKE GOD YOUR HOMEBUILDER

It is altogether possible that some who have read these

pages are completely disheartened. Never before have you known that God made such provision for parents. Never before have you heard answers to the questions you've had about child rearing and home building. Your children may have grown up far from your hopes and dreams for them. You may have put this book down and said, "Sorry, it's too late for me."

The problem with parenting is that when we finally feel prepared, we're out of a job.

1. Parent with Spirit-Controlled Power

Remember that God always starts with us where we are. Whatever your age or dilemma, you should remember His promise: "Draw near to God and He will draw near to you" (James 4:8). Make every effort to relate to all your children and grandchildren in loving recognition of who they are in God's sight.

Unfortunately, our parental zeal sometimes pushes us in the direction of quick fixes. Let me illustrate. In the 1800s the ranchers and farmers of the Southwest imported tamarisk (or salt cedar) trees into the Sonoran desert to prevent erosion and provide windbreaks. It seemed like a good idea—but they were to learn otherwise. One tamarisk bush produces about a half-million seeds annually. Each tree drinks up to 200 gallons of water a day and leaches important minerals from the soil. It wasn't long before plants started to die, salt deposits appeared, insects became homeless, and birds, reptiles and mammals had no food.

We face a generation of overly indulged children who are allowed to follow their own immature instincts. As parents we must seek balance and not cower in the face of our children's displeasure, not fear their threats or bow to their commands with impulsive, quick-fix actions. We cannot ignore Proverbs 1:8: "Hear, my son, your father's instruction, and do not forsake your mother's teaching ... ."

Let us neither over-parent our children nor shrink from the task. Are you frustrated, scared, don't know what to do? Just know that this anxiety never came from God. Reflect on this comforting capsule of Scripture: "For God has not given us a spirit of timidity, but of power and love and discipline" (2 Timothy 1:7). There is no place for cowardice when we have His never-ending source of power, love, and self-control.

I have found that feelings of competence are in direct proportion to the age of one's children. As a new parent, at first it seemed I could do nothing wrong. Then my first child reached age 12 and it seemed I could do nothing right! The problem with parenting is that when we finally feel prepared, we're out of a job. The truth is, the sooner we come to grips with the reality that our need for God is not partial but *total*, the sooner we will truly enjoy parenting.

2. Parent with Loving Humility

This priceless treasure we hold, so to speak, in a common earthenware jar—to show that the splendid power of it belongs to God and not to us. We are handicapped on all sides, but we are never frustrated; we are puzzled, but never in despair. We are persecuted, but we never have to stand it alone: we may be knocked down but we are never knocked out! Every day we experience something of the death of the Lord Jesus, so that we may also know the power of the life of Jesus in these bodies of ours. (2 Corinthians 4:7–10, PH)

Notice that "the treasure" is a common earthenware jar—like a peanut-butter jar—in order to prove to the world that the ability is not ours, but God's.

God's love "has been poured out within our hearts through the Holy Spirit" (Romans 5:5). Human love is conditional; divine love is unconditional.

If a mother says, "Stevie, if you don't do what Mommy tells you, then Mommy won't love you," she is selling her love too cheaply. As parents, we are always to love our children, no matter what they do. We may not like their behavior; but we are always to love them. That's where true love, *God's unconditional love,* comes in. The Bible says that while we were yet sinners, Christ died for us (Romans 5:8). That's unconditional love! God knows us totally, yet accepts us completely. And this quality of love for us, (His children) is our model for the quality of love and acceptance we must give our children.

In other words, "We love, because He first loved us" (1 John 4:19).

The constant reminder that our children belong to God before they belong to us should settle parents into a sober posture of stewardship. Every day the question should be flashing in the mind of a parent, "Lord, what should I do—or say—now for this child?" Total dependency on God is the secret.

Throughout the wisdom literature of the Bible there is a strong emphasis on parents and grandparents instructing children. The psalmist prayed, "... O God, do not forsake me, Until I declare Thy strength to this generation" (Psalm 71:18). How to do that?

• Know what the Bible teaches and integrate it into your own life.

• From their earliest years, teach your children God's love and His sovereign rule over all.

• Study your children's environment to identify major factors influencing their lives.

• Watch closely for each individual child's personality to develop. Listen more than you talk.

• Expose your children to every possible reinforcement and encouraging influence.

• Remind your children frequently that the Lord loves them far more than you ever could ... and that all actions are weighed by Him.

• You are the primary role model for your children: Live a life of moral and ethical excellence.

• Pray diligently for your children and accept God's plan for them.

3. Parent with Inner Peace

Discipline, or as some translations put it, self-control, is the fruit of the Holy Spirit. Self-control is linked to inner peace—and that is ready for our taking. "Let the peace of Christ rule in your hearts," writes Paul (Colossians 3:15). The parent who is ruled by God's peace will have little trouble displaying self-control. So, if Christ is controlling your life, you are in position to properly guide the lives of your children.

The secret of a disciplined child is a controlled parent.

Power, love, and self-control. These are the gifts God has given. They are also the prerequisites for the kind of parenthood that produces children who are a true reward. Like all of God's gifts, they are always good and always available because He never changes (James 1:17). We change, however. We are up and down, in and out, hot and cold, making it and losing it. Yet God does not mock us. He does not play games, laughing and saying, "Ha! You didn't make it!" Rather, He lovingly and generously provides all that is required for our needs as parents.

PREPARE CHILDREN TO SLAY GIANTS

It's evident from his encounter with Goliath that young David had received a lifetime of preparation. Although the youngest of eight sons, he knew what it was to assume responsibility. He was out working, in fact, when the big job opportunity came along. Keeping sheep in Palestine in those days was dangerous and often boring. The shepherd had to be resourceful and creative.

David had repeatedly faced and overcome the wild beasts that preyed on his flock. Undoubtedly he had known fear and uncertainty. But, alone with his responsibility, he had resisted, withstood, and killed the mountain animals with his bare hands. He had become physically strong and adept. He had practiced his musical skills. Most important, he had internalized the teaching of his father about the might and majesty of Jehovah. There was no ambivalence on David's part when he volunteered for the showdown with Goliath. He knew what he believed and why he believed it.

We indeed can ready our children for the present and future giants in their lives.

He was prepared. He was ready. And against incredible odds, he won!

Let me remind every parent that our homes are job #1. There exists no better preparation for living in our dissonant and hostile world than the Christian home. It is God's state-of-the-art make-ready place to produce winners for the battles of life. All the necessary tools are ready and waiting. The apostle Peter expressed it this way: "His divine power has given us everything we need for life and godliness ... ." (2 Peter 3:1, NIV). With confidence let us put these assets to work and tell the world the truth about how great is our God.

May heaven help *your* home today.

Your Life Journey

To help you apply this book's principles for building a harmonious Christian home, we have provided the following questions for your self-evaluation. Please reflect on them thoughtfully and prayerfully, then put your answers to work in your home relationships. For even more insight, after you've answered each question directed to you, ask your spouse and older children to answer them in a one-on-one or family-discussion setting.

FOR MOMS: HOW ARE YOU DOING?

1. Are you nice to come home to? When you are away, does the family look forward to your return with anticipation? Think of three reasons why they do—or should.

2. How do you keep up-to-date on the current concerns and joys of each family member without "prying"?

3. How can you better determine and help meet the emotional needs of each family member?

4. Although the father is the biblically designated spiritual head of the home, what contributions can

you make to the spiritual health of your home? If you are a single mom, what specific strategies are you utilizing to provide your home with spiritual "headship"? Do they seem to be working? What might you be able to do better?

5. What are you doing to keep yourself in good health? What could you do better? Come up with at least five ways you could combine regular fitness activity with quality time with your husband and/or children.

6. What personal interests outside the home and family have you cultivated?

7. If you are married, what steps do you take to keep communication open between yourself and your husband? If you are a single parent, gauge your relationship and that of your children with their father. What could you do to improve the relationship for your children's sake?

8. When you correct a child for wrongdoing, do you try to understand why the child did what he or she did? Do you communicate clearly with the child why punishment is necessary, and assure him or her of your love following the punishment?

9. Do your children know, beyond a doubt, that you love their father? What can you do better to be sure they have this confidence?

10. What are you doing to prepare your children and yourself for the "giants" they will face as they grow to young adulthood? What areas do you need to be sure to address in the near future?

For Dads: How Are You Doing?

1. Are you more positive than negative? Do your children think of you as a "don't-do-that" dad or as a "let's-do-this" dad?

2. In what way(s) do you actively teach your children scriptural principles of living (e.g., the fruit of the Spirit: love, joy, peace, patience, kindness, goodness, faithfulness, gentleness, self-control)?

3. Are your children proud of you? Why or why not?

4. What are you doing to keep yourself in good health? What could you do better? Come up with at least five ways you could combine regular fitness activity with quality time with your wife and/or children.

5. When you correct a child for wrongdoing, do you try to understand why the child did what he or she did? Do you communicate clearly with the child why punishment is necessary, and assure him or her of your love following the punishment?

6. Are you an involved or absent father? What would your wife say, and why? What would your children say, and why?

7. In what ways do you show your children the same love and forgiveness that God shows you?

8. Do your children know, beyond a doubt, that you love their mother? What can you do better to be sure they have this confidence?

9. What practical means do you use to communicate to each of your children that you believe in them?

10. Review in your mind the evidences of change in your life that the Holy Spirit has brought about. Now think of two more areas in which you want Him to work, beginning now.

For Families: How Are You Doing?

1. Which areas of our home life need the most improvement?

2. Which specific contributions to our home life do we want to make individually? (Each family member makes his or own list—changes in attitude, decisions to be made, specific projects, etc.).

3. What family goals shall we set (use of time, social goals, spiritual goals, etc.)?

4. What are the problems or hindrances we will face in attaining these goals? What specific changes will we need to make in order to accomplish these goals? How can we support one another in the process?

5. What is the divine promise in Philippians 4:19? How does this promise relate to our plans?

6. What are some specific ways we can be a positive witness to our neighbors?

7. Let's think of twelve fun family activities we want to do together in the next twelve months.

CHECKLIST FOR REMODELING YOUR HOUSE INTO A HOME

- Review the status of all members of your household to make sure everyone feels they are "VIPs" in the family.

- Check the basic structure. Dad is to be the head, Mom is to support him, and all the children are to share responsibilities.

- Scrutinize family values. A dominant, unifying, focal theme is needed. Anything other than Jesus Christ is too weak for permanent cohesion. A personal commitment to Christ, backed up with positive reasons, should be the parental example. At some point, every family member should be given clear opportunity to accept Jesus Christ as personal Savior and Lord.

- Develop family pride through accomplishment. Plant the seeds of positive self-esteem through music lessons, hobbies, good books, and other resources. Use every ability God gave you.

- Build up the fun side of the family. Be willing to laugh at your mistakes and develop imaginative, recreational pastimes. A positive, constructive home is magnetic.

- Ease up on forced togetherness. Encourage each family member to be away sometimes. At home, provide privacy to facilitate family members' personal relationship with God.

- Overhaul the emotional air-conditioning system. Avoid charging the atmosphere with tension. Keep the home ventilated with positive comments and relaxed attitudes.

- Sweep out old grudges as you would worthless debris. Forgive and forget the past, "even as Christ has forgiven you."

- Allow and even encourage the freedom to fail.

- Encourage open, honest, positive communication. A free exchange of ideas, without condemnation, is essential. Remember that communication is largely by life, not lecture.

- Keep the door open to family friends, allowing the fragrance of a virile Christian home to benefit others.

- Expect periodic spills of immaturity and imperfection. Clean them up with firm, calm, reasonable discipline. Plan a "better way" for next time.

- Allow the Holy Spirit to make you authentically like Christ. No artificial front can stand the daily erosion of home life. What you are is far more important than what you say.